How to . . .

get the most from your

COLES NOTES

 ## Key Point

Basic concepts in point form.

 ## Close Up

Additional hints, notes, tips or background information.

 ## Watch Out!

Areas where problems frequently occur.

 ## Quick Tip

Concise ideas to help you learn what you need to know.

 ## Remember This!

Essential material for mastery of the topic.

COLES NOTES

Your Guide to ...

Speed Reading

Read faster

Improve comprehension

Find what you need

to know — fast!

© Copyright 2003 Published by
COLES PUBLISHING. A division of Prospero Books
Toronto - Canada
Printed in Canada

Cataloguing in Publication Data

Sharkey, John, 1943–

Your guide to—speed reading:
read faster, improve comprehension, find what you need to know - fast

(Coles notes) Includes bibliographical references. ISBN 0-7740-0580-7

1. Speed Reading. I. Title. II. Series

LB1050.54.S52 1998   428.4'32   C98-930858-8

Publisher: Nigel Berrisford
Editing by Paul Kropp Communications
Book design by Karen Petherick, Markham, Ontario
Layout by Richard Hunt

Manufactured by Webcom Limited
Cover finish: Webcom's Exclusive DURACOAT

Contents

Introduction

Despite computers, videos and the Internet – or maybe because of them – more and more print is coming at us each day. Some experts believe that more written information has been produced in the last 50 years than over all of human history. And all this print has to be stored, read, understood and sometimes remembered for us to succeed at school or in our jobs.

Sometimes, coping with that avalanche of information will seem difficult, indeed. The average worker in a middle-level job is expected to read over a million words each week. It is little wonder that many people feel overwhelmed by the amount of information they are expected to absorb.

But there is good news. There are time-tested techniques for improving your reading speed and comprehension that will help you take control of the situation. All you really need is the desire and motivation to improve your reading speed and your skills in handling print.

Benefits you'll gain from the easy-to-learn speed-reading techniques outlined in this book include:

- an increase in your overall reading speed
- an increase in your comprehension rate
- an improvement in the amount you remember and the length of time you remember it
- relief from stress
- increased reading enjoyment

This book is for those people who are trying to manage the information overload that characterizes our times: students who must cope with large amounts of course reading, as well as working people who are being inundated with information that must be dealt with quickly and efficiently. If you are prepared to spend a minimum amount of time learning and practicing the reading habits described here, you will gain more control of your life and your reading.

CHAPTER ONE

Preconditions

The speed-reading techniques in this book have been developed by many different reading experts over the last 50 years. The work of Evelyn Wood and other educators has shown that learning a few simple techniques makes it possible to increase both reading speed and comprehension. Although the experts disagree on specific methods and approaches, they all agree that the mental attitude an individual brings to the task is critical to learning new reading habits and skills. As you will see, while it is relatively easy to learn new skills, it requires considerable commitment and concentration to integrate these techniques on a regular basis into your everyday work habits.

 The four essentials for speed reading are:
Positive attitude
Desire to improve
Willingness to learn new skills
Commitment to practice

POSITIVE ATTITUDE

Developing a positive attitude is essential to improving your reading rate. Lay your reservations aside and commit yourself to practicing the skills described in this book. Speed reading is like any other skill, the more you practice, the better you will become. It can be done and you can do it!

DESIRE TO IMPROVE

Just by picking up this book and reading this far you have demonstrated a commitment to improvement. You may be motivated by a desire to cope with a heavy reading load at school, or you may want to accomplish more at work. Whatever the reason, if you want to increase your reading rate, you must maintain a strong desire to do better.

COMMITMENT TO PRACTICE

This book is full of methods, useful hints and suggestions for improving your reading speed and comprehension. They are easy to explain and easy to do. What is more difficult is to integrate these techniques into your life and replace sloppy reading habits formed in childhood. Above all, you must be willing to practice these new techniques regularly and conscientiously, particularly during the learning phase. As with any new endeavor, repeated practice is essential to perfect new skills. In the case of speed reading, surprisingly little time is required. All you need is 15 to 20 minutes a day for concentrated practice.

Although it is preferable to practice in your regular study area, you can also apply your new skills on the bus or standing in a lineup, in fact almost anywhere you have a few extra minutes. This regular practice will enable you to replace your present reading habits with new ones. If you make a commitment to practice consistently for three weeks to a month, both your reading speed and your comprehension will increase dramatically. After that, applying these simple reading methods to everything you read will maintain these skills for a lifetime.

READING AND COMPREHENSION

Most reading experts agree reading and comprehension are the same thing. You do not really master one without the other. While it is often possible to "read" material in a language close to our own that we do not understand, this is not reading in a realistic sense because we do not understand the meaning behind the words. On the other hand, we have all tried to read an article in our own language that was incomprehensible because the author used a specialized or technical vocabulary. This can happen even when we recognize all the words and have some sense of their meaning.

Proper reading, however, only occurs when we have a high level of understanding of what it is we are reading. For this reason, all the reading exercises in this book are followed by short exercises to help you evaluate your comprehension of the text.

It is often assumed that increasing reading rate will decrease comprehension. In fact, just the opposite happens. Many reading programs and tests have shown that increased reading rates accompanied by a change in reading habits also increases comprehension. Initially, while these techniques are being learned and practiced, there may be a drop in your understanding, but comprehension quickly picks up again and even increases as the new reading habits become ingrained.

CALCULATING YOUR READING RATE

The first thing to do is to calculate your current reading rate. This will provide the necessary benchmark by which to evaluate your progress through this book and the accompanying exercises.

A short story, broken into sections, has been selected for your first speed-reading exercises. The built-in reader appeal of narrative fiction makes it appropriate material for learning new reading skills. Each selection will be followed by five short questions to test your comprehension.

The only material you need is a pen, paper and a timer to calculate your reading rate. This can be either a watch with a second hand or counter, or a device such as an electronic egg timer. If you use a timer, make sure it does not tick as this can be distracting while you read.

Read this exercise at your usual reading speed. Don't try to speed up or concentrate any harder than you normally do.

Reading exercise #1

Start timer now.

An Occurrence at Owl Creek Bridge, by Ambrose Bierce

A man stood upon a railroad bridge in northern Alabama, looking down into the swift water 20 feet below. The man's hands were behind his back, the wrists bound with a cord. A rope closely encircled his neck. It was attached to a stout cross-timber above his head and the slack fell to the level of his knees. Some loose boards laid upon the ties supporting the rails of the railway supplied a footing for him and his executioners – two private soldiers of the Federal army, directed by a sergeant who in civilian life may have been a deputy sheriff.

At a short remove upon the same temporary platform was an officer in the uniform of his rank, armed. He was a captain. A sentinel at each end of the bridge stood with his rifle in the position known as "support," that is to say, vertical in front of the left shoulder, the hammer resting on the forearm thrown straight across the chest – a formal and unnatural position, enforcing an erect carriage of the body. It did not appear to be the duty of these two men to know what was occurring at the center of the bridge; they merely blockaded the two ends of the foot planking that traversed it.

Beyond one of the sentinels nobody was in sight; the railroad ran straight away into a forest for a hundred yards, then, curving, was lost to view. Doubtless there was an outpost farther along. The other bank of the stream was open ground – a gentle slope topped with a stockade of vertical tree trunks, loopholed for rifles, with a single embrasure through which protruded the muzzle of a brass cannon commanding the bridge. Midway up the slope between the bridge and fort were the spectators – a single company of infantry in line, "at parade rest," the butts of their rifles on the ground, the barrels inclining slightly backward against the right shoulder, the hands crossed upon the stock. A lieutenant stood at the right of the line, the point of his sword upon the ground, his left hand resting upon his right. Excepting the group of four at the center of the bridge, not a man moved. The company faced the bridge, staring stonily, motionless. The sentinels, facing the banks of the stream, might have been statues to adorn the bridge. The captain stood with folded arms, silent, observing the work of his subordinates, but making no sign.

Death is a dignitary who, when he comes announced, is to be received with formal manifestations of respect, even by those most familiar with him. In the code of military etiquette silence and fixity are forms of deference.

The man who was engaged in being hanged was apparently about 35 years of age. He was a civilian, if one might judge from his habit, which was that of a planter. His features were good – a straight nose, firm mouth, broad forehead, from which his long, dark hair was combed straight back, falling behind his ears to the collar of his well-fitting frock coat. He wore a moustache and pointed beard, but no whiskers; his eyes were large and dark grey, and had a kindly expression which one would hardly have expected in one whose neck was in the hemp. Evidently this was no vulgar assassin. The liberal military code makes provision for hanging many kinds of persons, and gentlemen are not excluded.

The preparations being complete, the two private soldiers stepped aside and each drew away the plank upon which he had been standing. The sergeant turned to the captain, saluted and placed himself immediately behind that officer, who in turn moved apart one pace. These movements left the condemned man and the sergeant standing on the two ends of the same plank, which spanned three of the cross-ties of the bridge. The end upon which the civilian stood almost, but not quite, reached a fourth. This plank had been held in place by the weight of the captain; it was now held by that of the sergeant. At a signal from the former the latter would step aside, the plank would tilt and the condemned man go down between two ties. The arrangement commended itself to his judgement as simple and effective. His face had not been covered nor his eyes bandaged. He looked a moment at his unsteadfast footing, then let his gaze wander to the swirling water of the stream racing madly beneath his feet. A piece of dancing driftwood caught his attention and his eyes followed it down the current. How slowly it appeared to move! What a sluggish stream!

He closed his eyes in order to fix his last thoughts upon his wife and children. The water, touched to gold by the early sun, the brooding mists under the banks at some distance down the stream, the fort, the soldiers, the piece of drift – all had distracted him. And now he became conscious of a new disturbance. Striking through the thought of his dear ones was sound which he could neither ignore nor understand, a sharp, distinct, metallic percussion like the stroke of a blacksmith's hammer upon the anvil; it had the same ringing quality. He wondered what it was, and whether immeasurably distant or near by – it seemed both. Its recurrence was regular, but as slow as the tolling of a death knell. He awaited each new stroke with impatience and – he knew not why – apprehension. The intervals of silence grew progressively longer; the delays became maddening. With their greater infrequency the sounds increased in strength and sharpness. They hurt his ear like the thrust of a knife; he feared he would shriek. What he heard was the ticking of his watch.

He unclosed his eyes and saw again the water below him. "If I could free my hands," he thought, "I might throw off the noose and spring into the stream. By diving I could evade the bullets and, swimming vigorously, reach the bank, take to the woods and get away home. My home, thank God, is as yet outside their lines; my wife and little ones are still beyond the invader's farthest advance."

As these thoughts, which have here to be set down in words, were flashed into the doomed man's brain rather than evolved from it the captain nodded to the sergeant. The sergeant stepped aside.

Stop timer.

How long did it take you to read the selection?

_____ (minutes, seconds)

Reading rate:_____ (see next page)

Calculate your reading rate by:

- writing down how long it took to read the exercise in minutes and additional seconds
- converting that time into total number of seconds
- dividing the number of seconds into the number of words in the exercise – in this case 1065
- multiplying this number (which is actually the number of words per second) by 60 to get your reading rate per minute or "words per minute" (wpm)

Example

Reading time: 4 minutes 30 seconds = 270 seconds

1065 words ÷ 270 seconds = 4 (words per second)

4 x 60 = 240 wpm

Check the following chart to see how your reading rate compares with the average reading rate for people with different skills and education levels. If you are an average reader, your speed is between 150 and 300 wpm.

Grade 3 - 4 student	60 - 80 wpm
Senior-elementary student	120 - 180 wpm
High-school student	200 wpm
Average adult	200 wpm
University student	325 wpm
Graduate student	400 wpm
Average speed reader	500 - 1,500 wpm

Notice adult reading rates are the same as high-school students. This is true even for university-educated adults. Once people leave school or university, they stop reading intensively and their reading rate often goes down significantly.

Now answer the five true (T) or false (F) comprehension questions. Not mentioned (N) has been added to minimize the guessing that can take place with true/false questions. The correct answers are found in Appendix A. Give yourself 20 points for each correct answer and then total the result. This will give you an approximate percentage rate of comprehension for the selection. Put your reading rate and comprehension test results on the progress table in Appendix B.

Comprehension exercise #1:
Answer the following questions either true (T), false (F), or not mentioned (N).

1. The story is set in Alabama during the American Civil War.

   _____

2. Preparations are being made to execute a man by firing squad.

   _____

3. The condemned man could hear the ticking of his watch.

   _____

4. The condemned man was 50 years old. _____

5. The execution took place before a major battle. _____

*Comprehension rate:*_____

Congratulations! You have just taken the first step along the path to increasing your reading speed. You have shown motivation and commitment and you now have a pretty good idea of how well and how fast you read. It is time to move on and learn some practical ways to improve your skills.

CHAPTER TWO

The hand pacer technique

This chapter will demonstrate a simple technique that is the basis of speed reading in this book. More sophisticated variations of this technique are explained in later chapters and will help you read even faster.

WHAT IS READING?

Reading is a complex physical and mental process that is still not completely understood. At its simplest, reading is the process whereby the eyes recognize symbols which the brain translates into meaning. Of course, the brain does this with everything we see, or at least tries to. Reading takes place more effectively when the reader is able to apply prior knowledge to a specific reading context. Prior knowledge refers to our life experience in general, our knowledge of word meanings and sentence structure, and our understanding of relevant information. Furthermore, the definitions of specific words are not as important as their meaning in context with other words in a text. In other words, with reading, the brain processes letter symbols that have sounds associated with them. In a sequence, these become meaningful words or images.

The way we read is largely determined by the way we were taught to read. Many of us were told to sound each word out loud to the teacher or ourselves. We put our finger under each word and sounded it out phonetically according to the syllables. Then we went on to the next word. Some teachers and parents used flash cards with words. Students were taught to recognize these words on sight and say them out loud. These practices were kept up until about grade 3 when we were all supposed to be able to read. Although we may have been asked to read out loud in later grades, it was usually left to us to improve our ability through reading more demanding material.

In general, this process was successful for the majority of learners. At the same time, the reading habits we formed early in school often prevent us from reading quickly later on.

TYPES OF READERS

Readers can be divided into three general categories: physical, audio and visual.

Physical readers are people who have some part of their body in motion while they read. At one time or another we have all seen people twiddling their hair, tapping their feet or swinging their legs as they pore over a book. Stop their physical activity and these people literally cannot read. This type of reader is usually much slower than readers in the other groups.

Many people fall into the second category of **auditory readers**. This group says the words as they read them. Some people in this group literally vocalize the words out loud, either clearly pronouncing each word or mumbling or whispering the text as they are reading. Most people, though, say the words mentally to themselves as they read. This process is referred to as "subvocalizing." This is often a direct carry-over from the phonetic approach to reading we were taught as children. Most physical readers fall into this category as well. We will refer to both practices in this book as "vocalizing."

Some lucky people already recognize words by sight. These are **visual readers** who understand the meaning of words by looking at them. Like the lens of a camera, visual readers take in one to three words or more at a time and recognize what they mean instantly. Visual readers have the ability to visualize an image from what they are reading. This makes it easier for them to translate meaning from the printed symbols on a page of text. This group learns to speed read quickly and has fewer barriers to success. Included here are people who have been trained as speed readers as well as readers with photographic memories. They are able to absorb entire paragraphs or pages at a glance and understand what they see immediately. Partially because of their ability to see in images, they have an extremely high rate of recall.

Which group are you in?

These categories are not carved in stone: readers can change their type depending on the material they are reading or on the circumstances. For example, physical and auditory readers may not need to move, or repeat to themselves familiar words on street signs or place names. On the other hand, visual readers may have to vocalize text with which they are unfamiliar or which is especially difficult. Regardless of the type of reader you are, you can learn to speed read. It just takes a little longer and requires more practice if you are a physical or auditory reader.

This book has been written to train people to read faster by becoming well-trained visual readers. The simple technique outlined below will speed you on your way.

The pacer technique

- Lay this book flat on a hard surface.
- If you are right-handed, lightly place your right hand palm down on the page. Put the tip of your index or middle finger under the first word at the beginning of the selection.
- If you are more comfortable with a pen, pencil or other pointed object, use that instead.
- Whether you use your finger or some other object, this book will refer to it as a **pacer**.
- Use your left hand to turn the page when you need to.
- If you are left-handed, do the reverse. Use your left hand as the pacer and turn the pages with your right hand.
- Some right-handed people may prefer to use their left hand as the pacer and some left-handed people may prefer to use their right hand. There is no right or wrong way to perform this technique. The important thing is to choose the hand most comfortable for you.

This technique involves running your pacer under each line of text from left to right across the page. Focus your eyes just above and to the right of your pacer along the line of words. When you reach the right margin, bring your pacer smoothly and quickly back to the beginning of the next line of text and repeat the process. Practice this technique a few times so you can do it smoothly and comfortably.

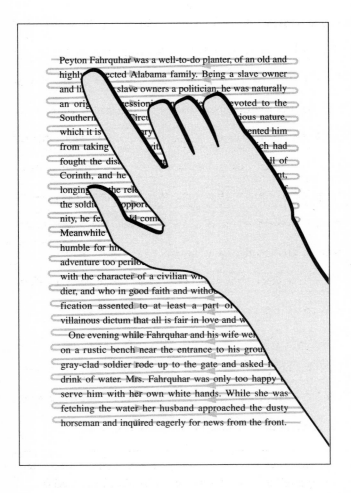

Now that you have practised the basic hand movement, the next step is to let your hand guide your eyes in a smooth, regular movement over the text. This will keep your eyes moving forward and eliminate the eye regression which always slows down reading.

The selection below is widely spaced with grey guidelines for your pacer to follow. Practise the technique here.

A man stood upon a railroad bridge in northern Alabama, looking down into the swift water 20 feet below. The man s hands were behind his back, the wrists bound with a cord. A rope closely encircled his neck. It was attached to a stout cross-timber above his head and the slack fell to the level of his knees. Some loose boards laid upon the ties supporting the rails of the railway supplied a footing for him and his executioners — two private soldiers of the Federal army, directed by a sergeant who in civilian life may have been a deputy sheriff.

At a short remove upon the same temporary platform was an officer in the uniform of his rank, armed. He was a captain. A sentinel at each end of the bridge stood with his rifle in the position known as support, that is to say, vertical in front of the left shoulder, the hammer resting on the forearm thrown straight across the chest.

For the next reading selection, use your new pacer technique to push yourself to read slightly faster. You'll be amazed that you can read 30 percent to 40 percent faster just by using your hand to guide your eyes.

Reading exercise #2

Start timer now.

An Occurrence at Owl Creek Bridge, (continued from exercise 1)

Peyton Fahrquhar was a well-to-do planter, of an old and highly respected Alabama family. Being a slave owner and, like other slave owners, a politician, he was naturally an original secessionist and ardently devoted to the Southern cause. Circumstances of an imperious nature, which it is unnecessary to relate here, had prevented him from taking service with that gallant army which had fought the disastrous campaigns ending with the fall of Corinth, and he chafed under the inglorious restraint, longing for the release of his energies, the larger life of the soldier, the opportunity for distinction. That opportunity, he felt, would come, as it comes to all in wartime. Meanwhile he did what he could. No service was too humble for him to perform in the aid of the South, no adventure too perilous for him to undertake if consistent with the character of a civilian who was at heart a soldier, and who in good faith and without too much qualification assented to at least a part of the frankly villainous dictum that all is fair in love and war.

One evening while Fahrquhar and his wife were sitting on a rustic bench near the entrance to his grounds, a grey-clad soldier rode up to the gate and asked for a drink of water. Mrs. Fahrquhar was only too happy to serve him with her own white hands. While she was fetching the water her husband approached the dusty horseman and inquired eagerly for news from the front.

"The Yanks are repairing the railroads," said the man, "and are getting ready for another advance. They have reached the Owl Creek bridge, put it in order and built a stockade on the north bank. The commandant has issued an order, which is posted everywhere, declaring that any civilian caught interfering with the railroad, its bridges, tunnels, or trains will be summarily hanged. I saw the order."

"How far is it to the Owl Creek bridge?" Fahrquhar asked.

"About 30 miles."

"Is there no force on this side of the creek?"

"Only a picket post half a mile out, on the railroad, and a single sentinel at this end of the bridge."

"Suppose a man – a civilian and student of hanging – should elude the picket post and perhaps get the better of the sentinel," said Fahrquhar, smiling, "what could he accomplish?"

The soldier reflected. "I was there a month ago," he replied. "I observed that the flood of last winter had lodged a great quantity of driftwood against the wooden pier at this end of the bridge. It is now dry and would burn like tinder."

The lady had now brought the water, which the soldier drank. He thanked her ceremoniously, bowed to her husband and rode away. An hour later, after nightfall, he repassed the plantation, going northward in the direction from which he had come. He was a Federal scout.

As Peyton Fahrquhar fell straight downward through the bridge he lost consciousness and was as one already dead. From this state he was awakened – ages later, it seemed to him – by the pain of a sharp pressure upon his throat, followed by a sense of suffocation. Keen, poignant agonies seemed to shoot from his neck downward through every fiber of his body and limbs. These pains appeared to flash along well-defined lines of ramification and to beat with an inconceivably rapid periodicity. They seemed like streams of pulsating fire heating him to an intolerable temperature. As to his head, he was conscious of nothing but a feeling of fullness – of congestion. These sensations were unaccompanied by thought. The intellectual part of his nature was already effaced; he had power only to feel, and feeling was torment. He was conscious of motion. Encompassed in a luminous cloud, of which he was now merely the fiery heart, without material substance, he swung through unthinkable arcs of oscillation, like a vast pendulum. Then all at once, with terrible suddenness, the light about him shot upward with the noise of a loud splash; a frightful roaring was in his ears, and all was cold and dark. The power of thought was restored; he knew that the rope had broken

17

and he had fallen into the stream. There was no additional strangulation; the noose about his neck was already suffocating him and kept the water from his lungs. To die of hanging at the bottom of a river! – the idea seemed to him ludicrous. He opened his eyes in the darkness and saw above him a gleam of light, but how distant, how inaccessible! He was still sinking, for the light became fainter and fainter until it was a mere glimmer. Then it began to grow and brighten, and he knew that he was rising towards the surface – knew it with reluctance, for he was now very comfortable. "To be hanged and drowned," he thought, "that is not so bad; but I do not wish to be shot. No; I will not be shot; that is not fair."

He was not conscious of an effort, but a sharp pain in his wrist apprised him that he was trying to free his hands. He gave the struggle his attention, as an idler might observe the feat of a juggler, without interest in the outcome. What splendid effort! – what magnificent, what superhuman strength! Ah, that was a fine endeavor! Bravo! The cord fell away; his arms parted and floated upward, the hands dimly seen on each side in the growing light. He watched them with a new interest as first one and then the other pounced upon the noose at his neck. They tore it away and thrust it fiercely aside, its undulations resembling those of a water snake. "Put it back, put it back!" He thought he shouted these words to his hands, for the undoing of the noose had been succeeded by the direst pang that he had yet experienced. His neck ached horribly; his brain was on fire, his heart, which had been fluttering faintly, gave a great leap, trying to force itself out at his mouth. His whole body was racked and wrenched with an insupportable anguish! But his disobedient hands gave no heed to the command. They beat the water vigorously with quick, downward strokes, forcing him to the surface. He felt his head emerge; his eyes were blinded by the sunlight; his chest expanded convulsively, and with a supreme and crowning agony his lungs engulfed a great draught of air, which instantly he expelled in a shriek!

He was now in full possession of his physical senses. They were, indeed, preternaturally keen and alert. Something in the awful disturbance of his organic system had so exalted and refined them that they made record of things never before perceived. He felt the ripples upon his face and heard their separate sounds as they struck. He looked at the forest on the bank of the stream, saw the individual trees, the leaves and the veining of each leaf – he saw the very insects upon them: the locusts, the brilliant-bodied flies, the grey spiders stretching their webs from twig to twig. He noted the prismatic colors in all the dewdrops upon a million blades of grass. The humming of the gnats that danced above the eddies of the stream, the beating of the dragon flies' wings, the strokes of the water spiders' legs, like oars which had lifted their boat – all these made audible music. A fish slid along beneath his eyes and he heard the rush of its body parting the water.

Stop timer.

Now, calculate your reading rate by working out the number of seconds it took you to read this selection, then divide this number into 1,265, the number of words in the selection, and then divide this number by 60 to get your words per minute. (See the formula at the end of Chapter one).

*Reading rate:*_____

How did you do? Probably, your rate significantly increased from exercise 1.

Comprehension exercise #2
Answer the following questions either true (T), false (F), or not mentioned (N).

1. Peyton Fahrquhar was a Confederate soldier. _____

2. Fahrquhar had been in captivity for four months. _____

3. Fahrquhar was told about Owl Creek bridge by a Federal scout. _____

4. If he was going to die, Fahrquhar wanted to be shot. _____

5. Underwater, Fahrquhar was able to untie his hands. _____

Comprehension rate:_____

Now calculate your comprehension. Did it go up or down? Most likely, it stayed about the same. However, if you did not do as well as you would have liked, don't worry. Your comprehension will improve as you become more familiar with the pacer technique.

This exercise should have shown that you can improve your reading rate. If you are really determined, you can improve much more. It lies within your power to become whatever kind of speed reader you wish to be.

While the exercises contained in this book provide useful speed-reading experience because the number of words in each has been counted, remember to practice your new skill in everything you do – including reading the text of this book!

CHAPTER THREE

Ordinary reading habits

Now that you have learned the essential reading technique for speed reading, it is useful to understand even more about the reading process. What you learn here will help you understand how you read, as well as the habits you have accumulated since you first learned to read.

HOW WE READ

The physical process of reading can be broken down into a number of different parts. English, like all the European languages, is read from left to right along a line of text. The eyes appear to move smoothly over the words, one line after the other. This is not quite what happens at all. In fact the eyes move in a **stop and go** pattern, stopping at certain points on the line and then rapidly moving to another spot.

To see this process in action, perform the following experiment with a friend or colleague:

- Take a printed sheet of paper and, with a pencil or pen, push a small 1/4″ (5 mm) hole in the middle. This hole is for you to look through.

- Ask your companion to read while you hold the sheet in front of your eyes at a distance where you are focused on one or both of the person's eyes.

- As the person is reading, watch his or her eye movements. You will see the eyes jumping back and forth in an apparently erratic manner along the lines of text.

Medical scientists believe reading only takes place when the eyes pause briefly at each stop along the line. It is during these pauses, or **fixations**, that the eyes register the words they are seeing and pass the information through to the brain for processing. The eyes act like duel synchronized cameras that stop and start so quickly they create the illusion of a continuous, smooth movement.

eye span   eye span

"The Yanks are repairing the • railroads," said the man,"and • are getting ready• for another advance. They • have reached the • Owl Creek

fixation point   fixation point

The number of words the eye registers on any given fixation is referred to as **eye span**. The eye span can vary considerably depending on the type of material being read. For difficult or unfamiliar technical information, the eyes may fixate on almost every word in a line. For less demanding material, the eye span may increase to four words. The average eye span is about two to three words. One of the objectives of this book is to train readers to increase their eye span to take in more words. The wider the eye span, the less your eyes will stop and the faster you will read.

COMMON READING HABITS

A common reading practice is the habit of going back over or rereading parts of the material already read. This habit of **regression** is one of the major blocks to faster reading. Average readers unconsciously reread about 25 to 30 percent of everything they read, reducing their reading speed by the same percentage. Many readers are convinced they absolutely *must* look back to ensure they understand what they are reading. In fact, there are those who believe they cannot read unless they can reread.

While there is considerable debate among speed-reading experts about the necessity of regressing, many speed readers do reread difficult passages occasionally to ensure comprehension. Still, there is a considerable difference between the conscious, voluntary regression of speed readers and the unconscious, involuntary rereading habits of ordinary readers. Regression always slows reading down. In the worst cases, regression can lead to confusion and boredom as slow readers often lose their train of thought and their place in the text.

Remember the reading exercises in the first two chapters and the substantial increase in your reading speed between the two? The main reason your speed increased so dramatically was that the technique used on the second exercise prevented you from regressing. By focusing on your pacer as it moved along, your eyes were prevented from going back over words or sentences you had just read.

Avoid regressing or rereading material already read.

Vocalizing, the habit of pronouncing – either out loud or to ourselves – everything we read, is one of the major obstacles to reading quickly. This is because it is only possible to speak out loud about 250 to 300 wpm and to vocalize (speak silently, to ourselves) at around 600 wpm. Anyone who wishes to become an effective speed reader must break the habit of vocalizing.

All the techniques and exercises in this book are geared to forcing you to read at speeds far beyond anyone's ability to vocalize. As you continue to practice, you will no longer have to vocalize the more common, smaller words. Soon, this will happen with bigger and bigger words. This practice is training you to understand what you are reading immediately, without saying the words first, just as you do when you see a photograph or a picture. The more you are able to visualize the material you are reading, the sooner you will stop vocalizing and the more quickly you will read.

You will read more quickly if you **visualize**, not vocalize, the words.

CONSTANT READING SPEED

One characteristic of slow readers is they read everything at the same speed. Yet not all material requires the same level of concentration. Accordingly, you must learn to vary your speed. If you are reading an enjoyable novel, you read it more quickly than you would read Einstein's Theory of Relativity, for example. To a certain extent, this depends on the individual. Physics professors may well read Einstein's theories, with which they are familiar, much more quickly than a novel they have little interest in. Having said that, most people will read a newspaper article much faster than they will a complicated macroeconomic analysis of international trade.

A useful way to visualize this point is to imagine a 600 km car trip. You've done the trip before and you know what to expect. You calculate the journey will take approximately six hours. That's an average of 100 km/h. But you know you never drive at a constant speed. Your speed will vary according to the road conditions you encounter. On a four-lane highway, you drive at 120 km or more. On a busy single-lane highway, you may average 50 km, while a 10 km stretch of road construction may slow you down to a snail's pace. However, your overall average is still 100 km and you arrive at your destination in six hours. It is the same with reading. You have to develop the skills to vary your reading speed depending on your purpose and the complexity of the material.

Vary your reading speed depending on the difficulty of the reading material.

In the last section of the short-story exercise, continue practicing the simple pacer technique you learned in Chapter two. Push yourself beyond your normal reading speed to increase your eye span and prevent regressions. Although it is too early for you to stop vocalizing by going faster, you will eventually overcome this habit as well.

Reading exercise #3

Start timer now.

An Occurrence at Owl Creek Bridge, (continued from exercise 2)

He had come to the surface facing down the stream; in a moment the visible world seemed to wheel slowly round, himself the pivotal point, and he saw the bridge, the fort, the soldiers upon the bridge, the captain, the sergeant, the two privates, his executioners. They were in silhouette against the blue sky. They shouted and gesticulated, pointing at him. The captain had drawn his pistol, but did not fire; the others were unarmed. Their movements were grotesque and horrible, their forms gigantic.

Suddenly he heard a sharp report and something struck the water smartly within a few inches of his head, spattering his face with spray. He heard a second report, and saw one of the sentinels with his rifle at his shoulder, a light cloud of blue smoke rising from the muzzle. The man in the water saw the eye of the man on the bridge gazing into his own through the sights of the rifle. He observed that it was a grey eye and remembered having read that grey eyes were keenest, and that all famous marksmen had them. Nevertheless, this one had missed.

A counter-swirl had caught Fahrquhar and turned him half round; he was again looking at the forest on the bank opposite the fort. The sound of a clear, high voice in a monotonous singsong now rang out behind him and came across the water with a distinctness that pierced and subdued all other sounds, even the beating of the ripples in his ears. Although no soldier, he had frequented camps enough to know the dread significance of that deliberate, drawling, aspirated chant; the lieutenant on shore was taking a part in the morning's work. How coldly and pitilessly – with what an even, calm intonation, presaging, and enforcing tranquility in the men – with what accurately measured interval fell those cruel words:

"Company!... Attention!... Shoulder arms!... Ready!... Aim!... Fire!"

Fahrquhar dived – dived as deeply as he could. The water roared in

25

his ears like the voice of Niagara, yet he heard the dull thunder of the volley and, rising again towards the surface, met shining bits of metal, singularly flattened, oscillating slowly downward. Some of them touched him on the face and hands, then fell away, continuing their descent. One lodged between his collar and neck; it was uncomfortably warm and he snatched it out.

As he rose to the surface, gasping for breath, he saw that he had been a long time under water; he was perceptibly farther downstream – nearer to safety. The soldiers had almost finished reloading; the metal ramrods flashed all at once in the sunshine as they were drawn from the barrels, turned in the air, and thrust into their sockets. The two sentinels fired again, independently and ineffectually.

The hunted man saw all this over his shoulder; he was now swimming vigorously with the current. His brain was as energetic as his arms and legs; he thought with the rapidity of lightning:

"The officer," he reasoned, "will not make that martinet's error a second time. It is as easy to dodge a volley as a single shot. He has probably already given the command to fire at will. God help me, I cannot dodge them all!"

An appalling splash within two yards of him was followed by a loud, rushing sound, **diminuendo**, which seemed to travel back through the air to the fort and died in an explosion which stirred the very river to its deeps! A rising sheet of water curved over him, fell down upon him, blinded him, strangled him! The cannon had taken a hand in the game. As he shook his head free from the commotion of the smitten water he heard the deflected shot humming through the air ahead, and in an instant it was cracking and smashing the branches in the forest beyond.

"They will not do that again," he thought; "the next time they will use a charge of grape. I must keep my eye upon the gun; the smoke will apprise me – the report arrives too late; it lags behind the missile. That is a good gun."

Suddenly he felt himself whirled round and round – spinning like a top. The water, the banks, the forests, the now distant bridge, fort and men, all were commingled and blurred. Objects were represented by their colors only; circular horizontal streaks of color – that was all he saw.

He had been caught in a vortex and was being whirled on with a velocity of advance and gyration that made him giddy and sick. In few moments he was flung upon the gravel at the foot of the left bank of the stream – the southern bank – and behind a projecting point which concealed him from his enemies. The sudden arrest of his motion, the abrasion of one of his hands on the gravel, restored him, and he wept with delight. He dug his fingers into the sand, threw it over himself in handfuls and audibly blessed it. It looked like diamonds, rubies, emeralds; he could think of nothing beautiful which it did not resemble. The trees upon the bank were giant garden plants; he noted a definite order in their arrangement, inhaled the fragrance of their blooms. A strange roseate light shone through the spaces among their trunks and the wind made in their branches the music of aeolian harps. He had not wish to perfect his escape – he was content to remain in that enchanting spot until retaken.

A whiz and a rattle of grapeshot among the branches high above his head roused him from his dream. The baffled cannoneer had fired him a random farewell. He sprang to his feet, rushed up the sloping bank, and plunged into the forest.

All that day he travelled, laying his course by the rounding sun. The forest seemed interminable; nowhere did he discover a break in it, not even a woodman's road. He had not known that he lived in so wild a region. There was something uncanny in the revelation.

By nightfall he was fatigued, footsore, famished. The thought of his wife and children urged him on. At last he found a road which led him in what he knew to be the right direction. It was as wide and straight as a city street, yet it seemed untravelled. No fields bordered it, no dwelling anywhere. Not so much as the barking of a dog suggested human habitation. The black bodies of the trees formed a straight wall on both sides, terminating on the horizon in a point, like a diagram in a lesson in perspective. Overhead, as he looked up through this rift in the wood, shone great golden stars looking unfamiliar and grouped in strange constellations. He was sure they were arranged in some order which had a secret and malign significance. The wood on either side was full of singular noises, among which – once, twice, and again – he distinctly heard whispers in an unknown tongue. His neck was in pain and lifting his hand to it found it horribly swollen. He knew that it had a circle of black where the rope had bruised it. His eyes felt congested; he could no longer close them. His tongue was swollen with thirst; he relieved its fever by thrusting it forward from between his teeth into the cold air. How softly the turf had carpeted the untravelled avenue – he could no longer feel the roadway beneath his feet!

Doubtless, despite his suffering, he had fallen asleep while walking, for now he sees another scene – perhaps he has merely recovered from a delirium. He stands at the gate of his own home. All is as he left it, and all bright and beautiful in the morning sunshine. He must have travelled the entire night. As he pushes open the gate and passes up the wide white walk, he sees a flutter of female garments; his wife, looking fresh and cool and sweet, steps down from the veranda to meet him. At the bottom of the steps she stands waiting, with a smile of ineffable joy, an attitude of matchless grace and dignity. Ah, how beautiful she is! He springs forwards with extended arms. As he is about to clasp her he feels a stunning blow upon the back of the neck; a blinding white light blazes all about him with a sound like the shock of a cannon – then all is darkness and silence!

Peyton Fahrquhar was dead; his body, with a broken neck, swung gently from side to side beneath the timbers of the Owl Creek bridge.

Stop timer.

Again, calculate your reading rate by working out the number of seconds it took you to read this selection, then divide this number into 1,432, the number of words in the selection, and then divide this number by 60 to get your words per minute. (If you need to, check the formula at the end of Chapter one).

*Reading rate:*_____

Comprehension exercise #3

Answer the following questions either true (T), false (F), or not mentioned (N).

1. A guard wounded Fahrquhar as he was escaping. _____

2. Fahrquhar was dragged under water by a vortex. _____

3. Fahrquhar was a prize-winning swimmer. _____

4. Fahrquhar was rescued by a troop of Confederate soldiers. _____

5. Fahrquhar was executed by hanging. _____

*Comprehension rate:*_____

CHAPTER FOUR

Speed reading habits

PASSIVE VERSUS ACTIVE READING

Now that you have learned something about the normal reading process and understand some of the habits that slow down the reading rate, it is time to start defining the new habits required to turn you into a well-trained speed reader.

To do this, you must change from being a **passive** reader to being an **active** reader. Passive readers read as if they were watching television, passively letting the words drift into their minds. Most of us read as if we were reading for pleasure. We read everything at about the same rate. Difficult material is slower and can often be reread a number of times – other parts, like a description in a novel, can be skimmed over lightly.

One way to become an active reader is to ensure you always read with a sense of purpose. Know what you are reading and why. This sense of purpose will increase your concentration, focus your attention on the material, help your retention and eliminate your regressions.

For instance, if you decide you want to read for entertainment or for the sheer pleasure of reading, you might curl up on the couch or in bed and read as quickly or as slowly as you want just for the enjoyment of the words or narrative. On the other hand, if you need specific information, statistics from an article or a careful analysis of a document, you must focus on your objective and vary your concentration and reading speed accordingly.

Always read with a **purpose**. Why are you reading – for pleasure, information or careful study?

CONCENTRATION

The single most important factor to increasing your reading speed and comprehension is the ability to focus all your attention on the text. Your whole body and mind must concentrate on the task at hand. Concentration is not a gift possessed only by the lucky few; rather, it is a skill that can be learned like any other.

You probably know what it feels like to experience total concentration. Most of us can remember reading a book we really enjoyed. As we got closer to the climax, we read faster and faster and turned the pages quickly. It didn't matter if we were in a crowded, noisy room, our eyes never left the page. All other considerations were completely blocked out, including an awareness of time.

Athletes know the importance of concentration in achieving their best performance. At the highest level of any sport, the players are all at roughly the same skill level. The ability to concentrate completely on the game often means the difference between winning and losing. A tennis player may refer to success in terms of concentration: "I was able to concentrate on my serve throughout the game in spite of the intense competition and the crowd." On the other hand, we may have heard a hockey player explain a poor performance by referring to a distracting injury that made it difficult to concentrate.

If concentration is a skill and not a gift, how can it be learned? It is easy enough to pay attention when we are engaged in something we enjoy doing, but what about an activity we must do for our studies or work? More specifically, how can good concentration skills for reading be learned? Four activities that will help to develop good concentration are:

- Organize yourself and your reading environment.
- Control distractions.
- Push yourself.
- Set time goals.

ORGANIZE YOURSELF AND YOUR READING ENVIRONMENT

Before you begin, make sure you have everything you need. This includes items such as a pen or pencil, paper, glass of water, etc. Ensure you have a good reading light with a 100-watt bulb. If possible, have some natural light coming from a different direction to cut down on glare. Make sure you are sitting in a firm, well-supported chair at a desk or table with a flat surface. Sit up straight with your arms loosely by your sides. Get comfortable, but not too comfortable. No slouching!

CONTROL DISTRACTIONS

Next, try to eliminate external and internal distractions. To a large extent, controlling the distractions in your personal space is a matter of individual taste. You might require relative silence in order to concentrate. In that case, turn off your radio, television and the ringer on your phone. If you concentrate better with music playing in the background, play something unobtrusive.

On the other hand, just because conditions are not ideal does not mean that you should not take every opportunity to speed read. If you find yourself in a noisy, crowded eating area with a few minutes to spare, try to block out the sound and focus on your text. It is important, of course, to select reading material appropriate to the situation. In a loud room, it may be more realistic to concentrate on a magazine or humoros book than on a complicated scientific theory. Whatever situation you find yourself in, try as much as possible to distance yourself, both mentally and physically, from the external distractions.

Internal distractions are often more difficult to deal with than external ones. Most of us have a list of activities we just have to do before beginning something we would rather avoid. Get these activities out of the way quickly. Go the bathroom. Get that essential cup of coffee. Make that important phone call. Then get down to reading. If something unavoidable comes up, do it immediately and get right back to reading. If the have-to-do task is avoidable, jot it down on paper and deal with it after you have finished your reading. Even if you are focused, your mind can often wander onto other subjects. Mentally pull yourself back to your reading. Tell yourself you will have more time to deal with these issues when you have finished your reading.

PUSH YOURSELF

The best way to focus your attention is to push yourself. Fast readers are active readers. People who can read at 800 wpm and higher have an energetic approach to reading. It is almost as if they pull the words off the page since they are so focused on what they are doing. The best way to get into this frame of mind is to continually force yourself beyond your regular reading practice.

SET TIME GOALS

Setting time goals for your reading greatly improves concentration. Be specific. Telling yourself you are going to read a book as fast as you can is too general. Instead, decide you are going to read for 10 minutes at 400 wpm, and then do it! Once you have set yourself a realistic time limit, you are more likely to accomplish your task and less likely to be distracted by daydreams or conversation. It is particularly important to set personal goals when you are learning new skills. After a few weeks of concentrated effort, this will become second nature. Setting goals gears you up for success. Your energy is up and you are ready to perform.

See how fast you can read the following passage, and how well you understand what you have read.

Reading exercise #4

Start timer now.

First Nations in Canada

Aboriginal peoples have occupied the territory now called Canada for several thousands of years. Many diverse and autonomous First Nations lived in the territory as hunters and gatherers for most of that period of time. The term "Indian," which outsiders long used to refer to First Nations peoples, is now considered a misnomer. "Indian" peoples in Canada today prefer to be known as First Nations. Canada's two other Aboriginal peoples are the Inuit and the Métis. Inuit are Arctic people. They have lived along the coastal edge and the islands of Canada's far North for thousands of years. Métis are people of mixed ancestry, the descendants of Aboriginal peoples who intermarried with European fur traders and settlers.

First Nations varied as widely as the terrain of Canada itself. In the wide Prairie interior, small groups of families co-operated in hunting the migratory buffalo which provided the meat and skins necessary for their survival. These people designed shelters to suit their nomadic existence. The tipi – a conical pole structure covered with skins – was portable, easily erected, warm, well ventilated and sound enough to weather strong winds.

The Pacific Coast First Nations, on the other hand, evolved a very different culture. The bounty of the sea – salmon, shellfish and the great whale – made possible the creation of permanent villages and leisure time to carve from cedar and stone magnificent art objects now housed in museums throughout the world.

Equally distinct and unique were the cultures of the nomadic Woodland people, the tribes of the British Columbia interior plateau, the Iroquoian farmers of southeastern Ontario and the hunters of the northern barren lands.

All of these cultures had in common a deep spiritual relationship with the land and the life forms it supported. According to First Nations spiritual beliefs, human beings are participants in a world of interrelated spiritual forms. First Nations maintain great respect for all living things.

With the arrival of European newcomers, this delicate balance of life forms was disrupted. In the 18th and 19th centuries, contact with Europeans began to change traditional ways of life forever. The introduction of firearms and diseases previously unknown to First Nations brought widespread devastation. For many decades, the Aboriginal population declined and the very existence of their unique cultures was threatened.

By the 1940s, First Nations leaders began acting to preserve what remained of their Aboriginal cultures, demanding that government stop exerting control over their lives. Through decades of dedication and persistence, First Nations have succeeded in making the government and the general public aware that they were once free, self-sustaining nations. Today, in seeking their own forms of self-government, they want to assume their rightful place in Canadian society. At the same time, they want to maintain the rich diversity of their traditional cultures which evolved over thousands of years before European contact.

Stop timer.

Calculate your reading rate according to the formula in Chapter one. The word count for this selection is 475.

*Reading rate:*_____

Comprehension exercise #4
Answer the following questions either true (T), false (F), or not mentioned (N).

1.   Aboriginal people are made up of First Nations, Inuit and Métis.

_____

2.   Pacific Coast First Nations lived in permanent villages. _____

3.   First Nation culture was unaffected by contact with Europeans.

_____

4.   First Nation leaders attend international conferences around the world. _____

5.   In recent times First Nations have had no influence on the general public. _____

*Comprehension rate:*_____

Enter your scores in the table at the back of the book. By now, you should be encouraged by the clear progress in your reading speed.

CHAPTER FIVE

Previewing

So now that you know how important it is to organize your-self, have the right mental attitude and practice setting time goals, what is the most effective approach to a reading assignment? What follows are some time-tested methods to help you read faster and increase your understanding of the material.

SKIMMING AND SCANNING

Two indispensable skills for rapid reading, and previewing in particular, are skimming and scanning a text to look for essential information. Both of these skills are closely related and are often confused, so it is important to get a clear understanding of their differences. Those who use these skills effectively can switch back and forth between the two as the need arises. Neither skill is read-ing in the strict sense of the word, but are useful to get to essential information fast.

Skimming helps you to look for the general ideas in a text. You skim by looking for key words and concepts that are the essen-tial core of a particular work. Depending on the text, you can get this information from the introduction, abstracts, chapter summaries and topic sentences usually located in the first sentences of paragraphs.

This technique works best if you run your pacer and eye down the middle of the text – without reading – concentrating on look-ing for the information you want. Amazingly enough, the information will often jump right out at you because you know where to look for it. The more you use this technique the more adept you will become at locating what you need in any text. Knowing the structure of various kinds of writing – as outlined in Chapter seven – will also help you get essential information as fast as possible.

If you don't find what you are looking for on your first pass, try running your pacer diagonally across the page from top left to bottom right. If you still can't locate what you are searching for, skim down the page from top right to bottom left.

Scanning is a technique that helps you look for a specific piece of information. This is a common practice many people do instinctively. For example, you are looking for a phone number of a friend whose last name is "Jones." First, you go through the phone book scanning for the Joneses. When you locate this section in the directory, you quickly scan for the section with the same first initial as your friend. Then you scan down this list until you locate the address you are looking for and the corresponding phone number. You keep the address firmly in mind as you scan, filtering out all other addresses until your eyes lock on the one you are looking for.

PREVIEWING

One way to read a book is to start at the beginning and work your way to the end. This is a common practice, but not a recommended one. Particularly for textbooks or other non-fiction, this can be like hacking your way through dense bush. You don't know where you are going and soon you don't know where you have been. After 50 pages, you put the book down and never pick it up again. There is a more effective way to approach a book, and that is to preview it.

Previewing is an important technique for effective reading. Essentially, it is a quick once-over of the reading material. Previewing can take anywhere from a few seconds to a few minutes to complete, depending on the length and difficulty of the piece. If done properly, this preview will give you the information you need to decide how to approach the work.

Contrary to the popular saying, you *can* learn a lot about a book by its cover. To make it attractive to buyers, publishers put as much information about a book on its covers as they can. As you preview, determine what the book is about and whether it is worth your time to read it.

Get used to asking yourself these questions:

- What do the title and subtitles tell me?
- Who is the author?
- Have I read any other book by the same author?
- If I have, what did I think of the author?
- What do I know about the publishing company? About this kind of book?
- What do I already know about the topic?

Check out the back cover or dust jacket. Look for a short summary of the book and a biographical sketch of the author. This way, you can discover a fair amount about the author, what the book is about and perhaps even why it was written.

Now open the book up and quickly leaf through the pages looking for the way it is structured:

- How is the book organized?
- Check out the table of contents, the index if there is one, the chapter headings and subheadings, and the charts, tables, diagrams, quizzes, glossaries, etc.
- How much of this do I want or need to read?

This preview should take no more than a few minutes and will provide you with a great deal of information.

If you decide this is a book you are interested in, take a few more minutes to preview it again. This time, pay particular attention to the introduction or preface. Quickly skim the opening and closing paragraphs of each chapter. These paragraphs often summarize the content of the chapter. This second preview will give you a feel for the author's style, tell you whether the information is well presented and easy to grasp, or difficult to follow. It should also confirm whether reading the book would be worth your time and effort.

Many people believe they have to read the entire book to get anything out of it. Nothing could be further from the truth! By asking pointed questions, it is possible to decide whether the book is worth reading at all. If you have framed your questions properly and know what you are looking for, you will be able to select only those parts of the book directly related to your needs and interests.

READING METHODS

The 1, 2, 3 method The simple **1, 2, 3 method** is a simple and effective technique for speed reading any text. The three steps to this method are:

1. Skim the material.
2. Read the material as fast as you can, marking any difficult sections.
3. Go back and reread the marked sections.

Step 1 As outlined during the preview process above, skim the text as quickly as possible to get as much information as you can. This is for an overview of structure and ideas, not for content.

Step 2 After the initial skim, go back and read the material at your fastest possible rate. Make sure you use a pen or pencil as a pacer so that as you come to difficult or confusing sections, you can draw a line along the margin for future reference. The number of marked sections will vary depending on the difficulty of the text. Scientific material will have more highlights than a sociology text. Don't worry about the number of passages you are marking but try only to highlight the really important ones.

Step 3 Once you have finished the second reading and marking step, go back and carefully reread those sections you have marked to make sure that you understand them completely.

Although it may seem that this method requires more time than a straight one-time-run through, in fact it takes much less. And you will have gone over the material three times concentrating on the important sections.

The SQ3R method Another popular way of previewing and reading a text is the **Search, Question, Read, Recite, Review method (SQ3R)**.

The first two crucial steps in this method are the same as those already outlined. Quickly go over the covers and front pages with specific questions in mind:

- What is this text about?
- Is it useful to me?
- What can I get out of it?

Stay focused on these questions as you skim through the text to see how it is organized and how it is written. Pay attention to the publication date, if this is relevant. For example, if you are looking for information on contemporary Russian politics, be suspicious of anything more than a few years old. If you are looking for computer information, get the most recent information possible. Always remember that it often takes a year for a book to be published, not counting the time it took to write it.

Read Now that you have a good idea what the book is about and what you want to get out of it, start reading as quickly as you can. Keep in mind the purpose of your reading as well as the questions you want answered. Concentrate on locating the main ideas and avoiding details. Don't worry if you find it difficult to distinguish between important information and supporting details. By practicing this method with a variety of reading materials, you will become increasingly adept at locating the central ideas. As you identify the important passages, mark them in some way so you can refer back to them later.

If the material is technical or scientific, spend a few minutes reading some essential definitions before you begin. This will help you locate the important ideas and make it clearer as you are reading. Any words you don't know, mark as you go along. When you are finished, go back to the glossary, if there is one, and look them up. Reread the passages containing these words to make sure you understood what you read.

Recite Summarizing out loud is the most effective way to retain what you have read. As you are going along, stop after each paragraph for a few seconds and review what you have read. You can literally say it out loud to yourself. The important thing is to make sure you understand the content.

The more you practice summarizing, the easier it will become. In a relatively short time, you will be able to increase the number of paragraphs you can summarize until you are doing entire sections.

Lay the book aside and make brief notes or develop a memory diagram as described in the next chapter.

Review Once you have read through the text quickly, go back over the material one more time. Do not read everything again but concentrate on the parts you have marked. Read these sections carefully and quickly, then add more details to your notes or memory diagram if need be.

DEVELOPING INTEREST

It is one thing to read material that you are interested in – it is quite another to work with material that you may just have to read for work or school. How do you motivate yourself to read material that you might rather avoid? Again a good approach is to ask yourself specific questions as you are previewing. For instance, ask yourself what you already know about the subject of the book. If the work is of general interest, you will be surprised at the amount of knowledge you already possess. Can you identify from your quick preview the author's angle or bias? How does this match up with what you know about the subject?

What you are doing is looking for ways to motivate yourself to engage with the subject. Try to develop questions about the material that relate to your interests. Keep these questions in mind as you are previewing, and as you are reading. Add these questions to your list of goals as you read through the work.

For example, a question you might ask about this book is:

- Am I convinced I can increase my reading speed?
- Will this book really help me to reach my goal?

Here is another exercise to help you practice the reading skills you have learned so far. See how fast you can read this passage, and how well you understand what you have read.

Reading exercise #5

Start timer now.

Killer Whales

Orcas or killer whales as they are more popularly known were, until very recently, possibly one of the most maligned marine mammals. Although they are the only cetacean (dolphin and whale) to live on warm-blooded animals, stories about their voracious appetites and treacherous natures have been disproved, thanks to the studies and observations of seagoing scientists and others. Numerous films have been made about their biology in the wild and there have been floods of popular articles written about them which have all helped to dispel old myths and make them better known than perhaps any other cetacean species.

There is no recorded instance anywhere in the world of unprovoked attacks on human beings by killer whales.

Killer whales have distinctive black, white and grey markings. Males grow to about 30 feet (9.1 metres) in length and females 26 feet (7.9 metres). Mature males have a dorsal fin of over 5.5 feet (1.7 metres) in height which is easily recognizable from a fair distance away. The dorsal fin of females is about half the height of the males. Immature males have dorsal fins similar in size and shape to females. Flippers are almost twice as large in males and flukes are also considerably larger. Weight is around 8 tons (7,200 kilograms) in full grown animals. Most animals have a light-grey "saddle" marking just behind the dorsal fin. The shape of this "saddle" differs in individual whales and is a useful form of identification.

Among the types of social groupings found in cetaceans, the killer whale pod is unusual. There is now extensive evidence that the pod consists of the same individuals (males, females and juveniles) which travel together throughout the year and over a period of at least seven years. The group is cohesive and travels close together, or in contact, along a broad front seldom exceeding 1.2 kilometers. There is a high degree of co-operation when hunting and ample evidence of communal concern. Typical pod size ranges from single to about 50 animals, though larger aggregations have been noted, especially in Antarctic waters.

Distribution is world-wide, but they are more abundant in Arctic and Antarctic waters where there is a never-failing supply of food. In some areas of the world killer whales appear to be migratory while in others they are apparently present all year round.

Killer whales appear to be opportunistic feeders and diet may vary from one region to the next or within a specific area. They are primarily fish eaters, but also feed on cephalopods and prey upon other cetaceans, seals and seabirds. It is of interest that killer whales appear to be selective in their choice and timing of food intake. They do not prey upon a particular species just because it happens to be in the same vicinity as they are. Whales, dolphins, seals and seabirds have been observed associating with killer whales on numerous occasions but they were not molested or attacked and the prey species appeared unafraid of the killers.

Killer whales are "super cetaceans" and do almost everything faster and better than other whales and dolphins. They are capable of swimming at speeds of 27 knots (50 kph) and can dive to a depth of over 1,000 feet (300 metres). They frequently "spyhop" (stand vertically with head and body, as far as the flippers, above the surface). This enables the whale to have a clear view of its surroundings. They "breach" (leap out of the water) and "loptail" (slap their flukes on the surface – a sound which carries for a considerable distance), and they navigate, herd their prey and communicate with each other by sophisticated sonar.

International whaling statistics indicate that killer whales have been harvested world wide but usually on a small scale. In the 1979/80 Antarctic whaling season the U.S.S.R. caught a total of 906 killer whales. Subsequent to this catch the International Whaling Commission banned factory ship whaling on this species. The meat is considered unfit for human consumption.

A number of countries have legislation to protect dolphins and whales in their 200 nautical miles economic zone. However, little international legislation exists to protect small cetaceans and they remain vulnerable to predation by humans for food, incidental killing in the fishing industry, pollution and ocean dumping. Since the early 1960s it has become fashionable to keep killer whales in captivity for public entertainment and "education." Many animal protection groups are against this practice and attempt to lobby their local governments to prevent killer whales from being put on public display.

Stop timer.

Calculate your reading rate according to the formula in Chapter one. The word count for this selection is 763.
*Reading rate:*_____

Comprehension exercise #5
Answer the following questions either true (T), false (F), or not mentioned (N).

1. Killer whales are voracious killers. _____

2. Male killer whales can grow to over 30 feet or 9 metres. _____

3. Killer whales travel in stable groups called pods. _____

4. Dolphins can swim faster than killer whales. _____

5. Killer whales are the most popular attraction at public aquariums. _____

*Comprehension rate:*_____

Enter your scores in the table at the back of the book. By now, you should be seeing clear progress in your reading speed.

Important questions to ask as you are doing your quick preview:

- What is the book about, or what is the main idea?
- What kind of writing is it, and how is it organized?
- Can I identify the author's purpose?
- Why am I reading this?
- How much of this do I need to read?

CHAPTER SIX

Speed reading techniques

In Chapter two, you learned the simple pacer technique that is essential to speed reading. Since then, you have practiced on a variety of reading materials. Now it is time for some refinements that will get you reading even faster. If you have been practicing with other material, you may have developed your own methods. As you increase your speed, it is important to push yourself even more. The objective, as always, is to stop involuntary regressing, and decrease dependence on vocalizing.

Start by making sure your reading material is properly prepared for effective reading. If you are working with a book, it should lie flat when it is opened. If it does not lie flat, and this is always the case with a new book, stand the book on its spine and gently push down the front and back covers by running your thumb or fingers along the inside edge. Now take a chapter or two, depending on the thickness of the book, from both the back and front, and do the same thing. Gently but firmly push the pages apart until they are lying flat on the covers. Continue this process until you come to the middle of the book.

HAND-EYE TECHNIQUES

A variation on the basic pacer technique is the **double line** movement. Instead of moving your pacer back and forth under each line of text, drop your pacer down two lines and read two lines of text at once. This will be difficult at first and you may feel your comprehension drop off. Keep practicing and it will become as familiar as the single line technique.

The invention of the potato chip

Potato chips were originally called Saratoga chips after the site of their discovery. In the late 19th century a Native American named George Crumb worked as chef for Moon's Lake House in Saratoga Springs, New York, where a fashionable crowd convened to take the waters of the spa. A persnickety guest reportedly disliked the cut of his French fries one night, and kept sending the oversized potato strips back to the kitchen for a more refined look. Crumb, finally exasperated by the guest's unreasonable persistence, decided to cut the potatoes just as skinny as he could. He boiled the slices in fat and presented them to the complaining diner, who was delighted and didn't think twice about the indecorous crunching and lip smacking and greasy fingers that accompanied their consumption. From this elegant dining room, the new and scarcely wholesome potatoes travelled throughout the nation, becoming one of the biggest selling snacks in America.

Once you become comfortable with this method, continue to push yourself more by using other techniques. Again, when you choose your reading technique, your first consideration should be the difficulty of the reading material selected and the speed at which you choose to proceed.

Zigzagging is a method particularly useful for easy text in columns. Start with the pacer at the top right of the page and, as the name describes, zigzag across the page, dropping down three to four lines at a time. As you are doing this, practice increasing your eye span as much as possible. Trace your pacer over the following sample to get a feel for the process.

Next try the **feather** technique, a variation of the zigzag method. Imagine the pacer is tracing the descent of a light object such as a feather that is floating down towards the ground. Of course, go much faster than a feather! You might be covering the same amount of material as the zigzag method but again, adapt it to your own preferences.

The Discovery of Champagne

The next time your find an excuse to break open a bottle of bubbly – be it New Year's, a wedding, or a whim – you might raise your effervescent glass in solemn thanks to one blind Benedictine monk who made it all possible. Three centuries ago there lived in northern France a great blender of wines, Dom Pérignon, who served as cellar-master at the Benedictine Abbey near Hautvillers for 47 years. For some reason that we may never know, this monk decided one day to seal his bottles with cork instead of the usual cloth soaked in oil. The carbon dioxide that is produced during fermentation could pass through the cloth, but was imprisoned by the new stopper. The result: a sparkling wine.

Dom Pérignon is generally credited with having put the bubbles into champagne. This is stretching his achievement a bit since growers for centuries must have noted that some wines re-fermented in the spring, and the New Testament speaks of wine skins splitting with new wine. But Dom Pérignon put his observations to good use, strengthening the bottles and tying his thick corks down with string. The people of the Champagne region of France, at least, have not forgotten their inspired monk. An annual wine festival in Hautvillers celebrates his name and his achievements.

Another variation is the **quest** or **circular** technique. The point, as always, is to push yourself to get as much out of the material as quickly as possible.

Clean water — life depends on it

What's in a glass, a sink, a river full of water? A refreshing drink ... a cleansing wash ... an invigorating swim ... a home for plants, insects, fish, birds and mammals? It all depends on the water quality.

We tend to think of water in terms of a particular purpose: is the quality of the water good enough for the use we want to make of it? Water fit for one use may be unfit for another. We may, for instance, trust the quality of lake water enough to swim in it, but not enough to drink it. Along the same lines, drinking water can be used for irrigation, but water used for irrigation may not meet drinking-water standards. It is the quality of the water which determines its uses.

Scientists, on the other hand, are interested in other aspects of water quality. To them quality is determined by the kinds and amounts of substances dissolved and suspended in the water and what those substances do to inhabitants of the ecosystem. It is the concentrations of these substances that determine the water quality and its suitability for particular purposes.

Drinking water, for example, is regulated by guidelines stringent enough to protect human health. Lack of such guidelines can lead to a variety of health problems. It has been estimated, for example, that contaminated water and poor sanitation cause 30,000 deaths around the world daily – the equivalent of 100 jumbo jets crashing every day!

Water is the lifeblood of the environment, essential to the survival of all living things – plant, animal and human – and we must do everything possible to maintain its quality for today and the future.

The technique to aim for is the "straight down the page" or **column** technique. You do this technique by running your pacer straight down the center of the page. Make sure you practice any new technique on something that is easy to read, such as newspaper or magazine articles. The narrow columns are ideal for this purpose. As you go, always remember to increase your eye span as consciously as possible. When you become proficient with lighter reading material, transfer this method to more demanding texts.

NOTE TAKING AND MEMORY DIAGRAMS

There are a number of techniques that are excellent for retaining information and improving comprehension and concentration. Underlining is the most common. If you are using a marker as a pacer, underline important aspects of the material as you are reading. After an initial preview of the material to get the overall sense, start again and underline all the main ideas and key points, as well as any difficult sections you encounter. This will enable you to focus immediately on the essential aspect of the text when you review it later.

Remember, only mark your own texts. Never do this with library books. It can be annoying and distracting to others who read the work after you.

The most effective techniques for remembering information are:

- Repeat the information to yourself mentally. Take a few minutes to summarize it in your own mind, going over the essential points and arguments.
- Repeat the information to someone else. Explaining something to someone forces you to be as clear as possible about what you know. If you are alone, summarize what you know into a tape-recorder.

- Write the information down. Putting it into your own words will force you to concentrate and organize your thoughts. This method is excellent for future recall.

One effective way to make notes is to use a "recall" or "memory" diagram. This can be any kind of design that is visual, logical and meaningful to you. Fill out the diagram with short descriptions of the essential information in your text as you are reading, or after you have finished.

Three of the most popular examples are:

- the tree branch
- the Mandala
- the box wheel

MEMORY DIAGRAMS

Tree branch

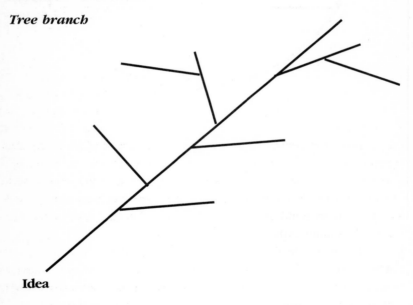

Idea

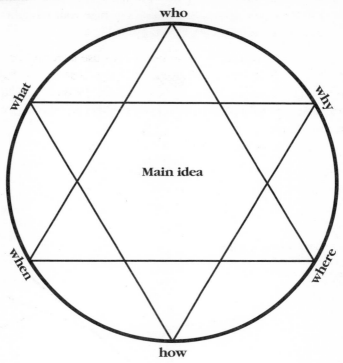

Place the central idea in the most prominent place in the diagram, either in the center or at the beginning if you are using the tree branch design. Once the central idea has been determined, reduce it to as few meaningful words as possible. Keep this central idea firmly in mind as you complete the diagram. Everything else you add should expand on the central idea.

Fill in the details by asking yourself the five Ws (Who? What? Where? When? Why?) and How questions. These are the primary questions that all good journalists answer in their articles. Answering these basic questions will force you to cover all the information you have read. As you add details, more details will come to mind. Add them as well. Make sure the subtopics and details are condensed into as few words as possible and capture what it is you are summarizing.

Here is an example of a box wheel memory diagram for the *Killer whales* reading exercise #5.

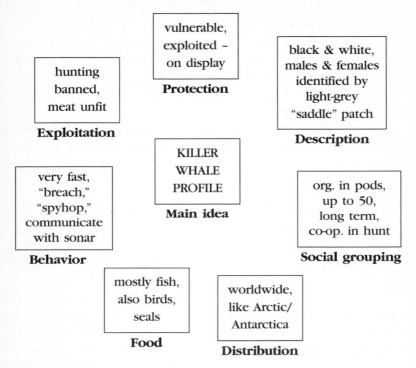

Reading aids

Various mechanical reading machines have been around since the ancient Greeks invented the **tachistoscope** ("swift viewing" in Greek) to help them cope with reading their awkward scrolls. Much more sophisticated versions of this machine were developed during World War II to help pilots identify aircraft. Essentially, it operated like a camera shutter, allowing images to flash at the viewer for a controllable period of time, often fractions of a second. This machine has been modified to take text slides adapted to various reading levels. By increasing the rate at which material is flashed at you, you can increase your reading speed.

A variation on the tachistoscope is the **eye-span trainer**, a small hand-held device that trains the eyes to take in an increasing number of words at a time. It can be adjusted to flash one to eight words, for varying lengths of time, from one-hundredth of a second to one second. This machine forces the eyes to see more at once and is a very effective way of expanding the reading span of your eye.

The **pace accelerator** is a desktop machine designed to take any kind of reading material. The pacer can be set to read at a number of settings or wpm. Most have a range between 200 and 2,000 wpm. Some more expensive machines can go up to 4,000 wpm. When the machine is turned on, a bar or beam of light slides down the page at a rate set by the viewer.

These devices are available in some educational stores and in some universities and public libraries. If set at a high enough reading rate, they are quite effective in preventing regression and forcing the viewer to stop vocalizing.

VIDEO CASSETTES AND COMPUTER SOFTWARE

Video and audio cassettes have replaced film as one of the latest technologies designed to teach speed reading. They are considerably more user-friendly than the older technologies, although they present the same information and techniques found in books.

In addition, an increasing number of excellent computer-software programs use digital technologies to teach speed reading. The better ones can be customized to accommodate everyone, from young readers to experts who wish to improve even further. They have the advantage of large databases of diverse exercises that can be customized to various age groups and language proficiencies. The programs use a variety of techniques for sight training. These techniques are similar to tachistoscopes and eye-span trainers and include numerous tests to eliminate standard reading problems.

While technical devices and software can be excellent tools for improving reading speed, they are most effective when used in conjunction with books on the same subject. As written material can be read almost anywhere at any time, it is still more versatile than information available from a screen. Although the mechanical and electrical machines are capable of increasing reading rates quite dramatically, these often drop back once the reader returns to regular print. The important thing to remember is the goal of increasing your reading rate and keeping it up without relying on any form of technical support.

Reading exercise #6

Start timer now.

The Origins of Halloween

Halloween is celebrated annually. But just how and when did this peculiar custom originate? Is it, as some claim, a kind of demon worship? Or is it just a harmless vestige of some ancient pagan ritual?

The word "Halloween" actually has its origins in the Catholic Church. It comes from a contracted corruption of All Hallows Eve. All Hallows Day, or All Saint's Day, November 1, is a Catholic day of observance in honor of saints. But, in the fifth century BC, in Celtic Ireland, summer officially ended on October 31. The holiday was called Samhain (sow-en), the Celtic new year. One story says that, on that day, the disembodied spirits of all those who had died throughout the preceding year would come back in search of living bodies to possess for the next year. It was believed to be their only hope for the afterlife. The Celts believed all laws of space and time were suspended during this time, allowing the spirit world to intermingle with the living.

Naturally, the still-living did not want to be possessed. So on the night of October 31, villagers would extinguish the fires in their homes, to make them cold and undesirable. They would then dress up in all manner of ghoulish costumes and noisily parade around the neighborhood, being as destructive as possible in order to frighten away spirits looking for bodies to possess.

Probably a better explanation of why the Celts extinguished their fires was not to discourage spirit possession, but so that all the Celtic tribes could relight their fires from a common source, the Druidic fire that was kept burning in the middle of Ireland, at Usinach.

Some accounts tell of how the Celts would burn someone at the stake who was thought to have already been possessed, as sort of a lesson to the spirits. Other accounts of Celtic history debunk these stories as myth.

The Romans adopted the Celtic practices as their own. But in the first century AD, they abandoned any practice of sacrificing of humans in favor of burning effigies. The thrust of the practices also changed over time to become more ritualized. As belief in spirit possession waned, the practice of dressing up like hobgoblins, ghosts and witches took on a more ceremonial role.

The custom of Halloween was brought to America in the 1840s by Irish immigrants fleeing their country's potato famine. At that time, the favorite pranks in New England included tipping over outhouses and unhinging fence gates.

The custom of trick-or-treating is thought to have originated not with the Irish Celts, but with a ninth-century European custom called "souling." On November 2, All Souls Day, early Christians would walk from village to village begging for "soul cakes," made out of square pieces of bread with currants. The more soul cakes the beggars would receive, the more prayers they would promise to say on behalf of the dead relatives of the donors. At the time, it was believed that the dead remained in limbo for a time after death, and that prayer, even by strangers, could expedite a soul's passage to heaven.

The jack-o-lantern custom probably comes from Irish folklore. As the tale is told, a man named Jack, who was notorious as a drunkard and trickster, tricked Satan into climbing a tree. Jack then carved an image of a cross in the tree's trunk, trapping the devil up the tree. Jack made a deal with the devil that, if he would never tempt him again, he would promise to let him down the tree. According to the folk tale, after Jack died, he was denied entrance to Heaven because of his evil ways, but he was also denied access to Hell because he had tricked the devil. Instead, the devil gave him a single ember to light his way through the frigid darkness. The ember was placed inside a hollowed-out turnip to keep it glowing longer.

The Irish used turnips as their "Jack's lanterns" originally. But when the immigrants came to America, they found that pumpkins were far more plentiful than turnips. So the jack-o-lantern in America was a hollowed-out pumpkin, lit with an ember.

So, although some cults may have adopted Halloween as their favorite "holiday," the day itself did not grow out of evil practices. It grew out of the rituals of Celts celebrating a new year, and out of medieval prayer rituals of Europeans. And today, it is only as evil as one cares to make it.

Stop timer.

Calculate your reading rate according to the Chapter one formula. The word count for this selection is 749.

*Reading rate:*_____

Comprehension exercise #6
Answer the following questions either true (T), false (F), or not mentioned (N).

1. Halloween comes from a corruption of the Catholic holiday called All Hallows Day. _____

2. Halloween is celebrated around the world. _____

3. Early Celts celebrated Samhain, an end-of-summer festival, on October 31. _____

4. Definite proof exists that early Celts carried out human sacrifices. _____

5. Turnips were used as the first jack-o-lanterns. _____

*Comprehension rate:*_____

CHAPTER SEVEN

Reading different types of material

As has been stressed in previous chapters, it is important to vary your reading speed according to the difficulty and importance of the material. Some of the factors that will affect reading speeds are:

- familiarity with content
- author's style
- sentence structure
- vocabulary

Again, your attitude and your purpose will also determine how you approach your reading. A strong motivation for specific information, such as research for a university essay, requires a quite different approach from reading for pleasure.

Another important factor to consider when deciding how to approach different material is to understand the structure of various kinds of writing. Knowing the structure of the material you are reading will help you plan how to read it quickly and effectively.

NEWSPAPERS

Newspapers contain four main types of articles: news stories, editorials, syndicated columns and feature articles. By far the most numerous are news stories, either written by local reporters or taken off wire services. These articles are structured in an "inverted pyramid" style, with the most important information at the beginning and the least important towards the end. In well-written news articles, the first paragraph or two always contains the answers to the six standard journalistic questions: Who? What? Where? When? Why? How? This enables the reader to read the first few paragraphs for essential details of the story and then skim the rest.

Editorials usually outline an issue in the opening paragraph, develop an argument throughout the body and end with an opinion or call to action. They are written by editorial staff and represent the point of view of the owners of the newspaper.

Syndicated columns are organized in the same manner, except the argument is more elaborate in the body of the article. These articles are usually written by well-known writers and often express personal points of view quite different from the newspaper's official position. For both editorials and columns, read the opening and closing paragraphs to get the essence of the issue and skim the body for the argument.

A super-quick way to read newspapers is to read only the headlines. These capture the essence of the content and can also reflect a point of view as well.

The fastest way to read newspapers is to skim with the "straight down the middle of the page" or column hand motion. As you read, keep in mind the structure of the article and recall what you already know about the subject so that you can skim over details that you needn't bother to read.

MAGAZINES

Magazine and newspaper feature articles have similar structures. The opening paragraph of a general-interest magazine is often referred to as the "grabber" or "teaser." Its chief purpose is to grab the attention of readers so they will continue reading the article. This "come on" can be in the title, or in an accompanying photograph. In the second paragraph, the writer says what the article is about and begins to develop a point of view. The midsection or body of the article includes facts, situations, examples and commentary. It is here the writer reveals the main arguments, uses examples and elaborates a point of view. The last section summarizes the opinion or argument developed throughout the body of the piece. It often alludes back to the opening teaser as a way to tie the article together.

Articles in specialized journals or periodicals are organized in essentially the same way. As a rule, however, they are less general in nature and more information-oriented than general-interest articles. They usually do not have, or need, an opening teaser to get the reader interested.

The quickest way to read magazine articles is to skim the title, subheads, photographs, the second paragraph, text boxes and other graphics. If the article interests you, quickly read through the body looking for facts and explanations, as well as the last paragraph for a summary of the content.

TECHNICAL AND SCIENTIFIC WRITING

Don't be put off by this kind of writing because you think it is too difficult to understand. Technical writing tends to be the most clearly written and well-structured writing around. It is most often written by knowledgeable experts whose principle objective is to make their subject as accessible as possible. Like scientific writing, the introduction will say what the material is about. The conclusion will sum it all up. Scan this material quickly to see if you wish to read more. Spend a few minutes looking up unfamiliar vocabulary. Reread it more slowly if you have an interest in the subject or if you come across difficult parts.

Like technical writing, scientific material is usually well organized and well written. Realizing that an enormous amount of scientific research is published annually, the scientific community has developed a standard whereby a short abstract of the article appears at the beginning of the work. This short précis gives an excellent summary of the material and makes it easy to determine if you need to read the entire article. In the case of a book, the introduction will give a clear summary of what is to follow in the body of the work. The last paragraphs summarize the work again, draw conclusions and make suggestions about future work.

Review the preview techniques outlined in Chapter five for a more detailed approach to this kind of material. The best way is to skim for essential details, speed read the body of the text, focus in on the abstract and conclusion, then reread again, paying particular attention to difficult sections and concepts. As you are reading, develop a memory diagram to help recall the material at a later time.

BUSINESS CORRESPONDENCE

In general, business correspondence tends to be short – about one to two pages on average – but there can be lots of it and the most important letters require some specific action.

Business correspondence can usually be sorted into three piles: IO, TA and BU. "Information only" or IO includes all the minutes of meetings, form letters, advertising material, product material and other items that might, just might, need to be looked at later. For now it just has to be filed. "Take action" (TA) is the one item in five or ten that needs to be handled immediately. Some people let this pile sit on the desk until each item is worked through. "Bring up" (BU) is material that will have to be dealt with later on, and should be set aside in a folder until such time as it needs tending. Organized people tend to their BU file at the beginning of each month.

Then there's the thinnest file of all: NMP – "not my problem." These letters get sent to somebody else for action and shouldn't be cluttering either your desk or memory.

With letters you decide to read, do a quick scan to find out who it is from. Check the letterhead, signature and title of the writer. This determines how much consideration to give it. If the letter is from an important customer, it will get more attention than if it is a form letter from a company soliciting your photocopying business.

As most business correspondence requires a specific action, scan for this as quickly as possible. It is usually located in the mid-paragraphs. Once the purpose of the letter has been determined, make a decision about what to do and then do it. Don't put off the decision until later, otherwise you may well end up wasting time rereading the material at a later date.

LITERATURE

The techniques outlined in this book are primarily designed to help the reader get essential information out of non-fiction material. Imaginative literature, on the other hand, is a different kind of reading. While it can provide considerable information on many subjects – think of the account of whaling in *Moby Dick*, for example – its primary objective is to provide its readers with a plea-surable experience. At its best, imaginative literature tries to entertain while it instructs the reader on a particular vision of the human condition.

This emphasis on pleasure and enjoyment derives from an appreciation of aesthetic considerations such as style, irony, humor, dramatic tension and suspense. Good literature also appeals to the senses. It is difficult to appreciate these features while speed reading a text for central ideas.

For instance, poetry and plays use highly concentrated language that is often meant to be read aloud. Much of the enjoyment of poetry comes from an appreciation of the way words sounded and are organized. It does not lend itself to being read quickly, although it is possible to skim longer poems after an initial slower read in order to recall content.

Narrative fiction is also read primarily for pleasure and aesthetic appreciation although, because the language of fiction is less dense, it is possible to read it much more quickly than poetry. Longer fiction is usually conventionally structured. The beginning develops the main characters and central issues and a longer middle section takes the central characters through a series of demanding difficulties. These difficulties are resolved in the ending or climax. This section can be followed by a short denouement, tying up any plot elements left unresolved by the climax.

There may be circumstances, such as preparing for a test, when you have to speed read a work of fiction. An effective approach in this case is to pay attention to the cover of the work. Most novels will provide a short summary of the story, without giving away the climax. This information will prepare you for the content. Think about the title and any short quotations at the beginning that provide insight into the author's intentions. Then read through the story as quickly as possible, using your pacer to prevent regressions. Set definite goals for the amount of time you are going to spend reading. As always, vary your speed depending on your purpose and the difficulty of the text. Descriptive passages can be skimmed over quickly, but pay close attention to longer speeches of significant characters. These often reveal the intent of the story. Make a memory diagram as you progress and re-scan the work when finished to fill in any details.

READING YOUR COMPUTER SCREEN

As computers become increasingly integrated into our work and daily lives we are spending more time reading information on computer screens. While this is unavoidable for material you are producing, prolonged on-screen reading is difficult and tiring. The best method for computer-screen reading is to skim and scan until material of particular interest is found, then download this material and speed read it as hard copy.

Sometimes it is impossible to avoid reading on screen. Here are some suggestions to make screen reading easier.

Make sure you are properly set up. Always sit in a proper chair adjusted for your height and weight in relation to your computer keyboard and screen. Most computer stores will tell you how to do this. Prolonged screen reading can place great stress on various parts of your body, particularly your eyes. Take frequent breaks and never work on screen for more than an hour at a time. Adjust the screen contrast to provide the best resolution for your work. Make sure your screen is not in front of a window and that you have appropriate light to prevent glare on the screen.

Use your mouse cursor as a pacer. If you've tried running your pacer underneath on-screen text, you know it will not be long before your arm begins to ache. While it is not a perfect substitute, you can use your mouse cursor as a pacer. The cursor speed and shape can be adjusted to your preferences and, although the cursor flicker can be distracting at first, with practice you can become quite effective at using it to pace yourself. Make sure whatever you have to read is single-spaced as the more dense the material is on the screen, the quicker it is to read.

Use the down arrow on your key board to control the speed at which text moves up from the bottom of the screen. This requires less motion than the cursor and you can vary the speed at which you scroll depending on your purpose and material.

Use the page down key. This key provides an entirely new screen of text at a time and is ideal for skimming and scanning. Move on to this technique after you have perfected the single-line spacer technique mentioned above.

Reading exercise #7

The following technical article describes the main features of the Hubble Space Telescope. Skim it quickly and purposefully, looking for information about what the telescope can do, who takes care of it and how it has performed.

Start timer now.

The Hubble Space Telescope

The Hubble Space Telescope (HST) was the flagship mission of NASA's Great Observatories program. Designed to complement the wavelength capabilities of the other spacecraft in the program, HST is a Ritchey-Chretien telescope capable of performing observations in the visible, near-ultraviolet and near-infrared range.

Placed into a low-earth orbit by the space shuttle, HST was designed to be modular so that on subsequent shuttle missions it could be recovered, have faulty or obsolete parts replaced with new and/or improved instruments and be re-released. HST is roughly cylindrical in shape, 13.1 m end-to-end and 4.3 m in diameter at its widest point.

HST uses an elaborate scheme for attitude control to improve the stability of the spacecraft during observations. Manoeuvring is performed by four of six gyros, or reaction wheels. Pointing can be maintained in this mode or the Fine Guidance Sensors can be used to lock onto guide stars to reduce the spacecraft drift and increase the pointing accuracy.

Power to the two on-board computers and the scientific instruments is provided by two solar panels. The power generated by these arrays is also used to charge six nickel-hydrogen batteries which provide power to the spacecraft during the roughly 25 minutes per orbit in which HST is within the Earth's shadow.

Communications with the satellite are maintained with other satellites. Observations taken during the time when these satellites are visible from the spacecraft are recorded on tape-recorder and transferred during periods of visibility. The spacecraft also supports real-time interactions with the ground system during times of satellite visibility, enabling observers to make small offsets in the spacecraft pointing to perform their observations.

HST was operated in three distinct phases. During the first phase of the mission, responsibility for the spacecraft was given to Marshall Space Center. This phase consisted of an extended, eight-month checkout of the spacecraft, including testing of the on-board computers, pointing control system, solar arrays, etc. This was followed by the Science Verification phase, lasting nearly another year, during which each of the six science instruments was tested to verify their capabilities and set limits on their safe operations during the remainder of the mission. Responsibility for the spacecraft during this second phase was given to Goddard Space Flight Center. The last phase of the mission, known as the General Observer phase, is planned to last through to the end of the mission and is the responsibility of the Space Telescope Science Institute.

The mission was troubled soon after launch by the discovery that the primary mirror was spherically aberrated. In addition, problems with the solar panels flexing as the spacecraft passed from the Earth's shadow into sunlight caused problems with the pointing stability. Steps were taken to correct these problems, including replacement of the solar panels, replacement of the Wide Field and Planetary Camera with a second-generation version with built-in corrective optics, and replacement of the High-Speed Photometer with COSTAR (Corrective Optics Space Telescope Axial Replacement) to correct the aberration for the remaining instruments.

Stop timer.

Calculate your reading rate according to the Chapter one. The word count for this selection is 501.

*Reading rate:*_____

Comprehension exercise #7
Answer the following questions either true (T), false (F), or not mentioned (N).

1. The Hubble Space Telescope (HST) can only perform in the near-ultraviolet range. _____

2. HST has photographed a super nova. _____

3. HST is modular to facilitate replacement of removable parts. _____

4. Two solar panels provide power for on-board equipment on HST . _____

5. HST was trouble-free from the moment it was deployed. _____

*Comprehension rate:*_____

Congratulations! The short technical article is quite dense but using the quick skim and focusing on specific information, you probably did quite well in your comprehension rate.

CHAPTER EIGHT

How to find information – fast!

Computer technologies have made more information available today than at any other period in history. There are over 50 million documents accessible – literally at our finger tips – through the Internet and millions of words are being added every day. While this information is an invaluable resource for people with computer access, it also presents ongoing problems about how to locate the specific information you need. Fortunately, whether you are writing a course assignment or researching a work-related project, there are people and technologies to help you locate information quickly and efficiently.

This chapter and Chapter nine assume the reader has access to a computer and is already familiar with basic software. A general knowledge of computers is an essential prerequisite to carry out any information search. Long gone are the days when resources could be found in library card catalogues.

Scanning and skimming are the primary reading techniques for searching online information. The most effective technique is to scan for the specific words that identify the material and ignore everything else. Only slow down when you find something potentially useful.

Do not spend time reading documents on screen unless you absolutely have to. If you are using computer terminals in a public setting, such as a library, it could be expensive or people could be waiting to use the machine. The most effective process is to scan as rapidly as possible, locate the information you are looking for and retrieve it in another format. This might include downloading material to be read offline at a more convenient location, printing it out on paper or retrieving a book or magazine from library shelves.

There are basically two kinds of information searches: specific and general. A **specific search** is one where you know the exact or close-to-exact information about: the author, title, subject or, if you are searching library databases, call numbers of the material you are looking for. You enter this information at the appropriate field prompt or into on-screen text boxes. Then the system does the search and tells you what material is available. Specific searches are the quickest route to information.

If you don't know the exact wording of the material you are looking for, or if you are researching a general topic, execute a **general search**. Think of this type of search as a funnel. It starts with a few general words to describe the subject area and is continually refined to achieve an increasingly narrow selection of material. Spend time refining your ideas to as few **key words** as possible. It will help you find what you are looking for quickly.

The main locations for rapid information searches are university and public libraries and the Internet. The rest of this chapter will focus on how to access information from libraries.

LIBRARIES – UNIVERSITY AND PUBLIC

University and public libraries are excellent sources of well-organized and reliable information. Easy access to online library databases is available through public terminals within the institutions or from remote computers using connection software. Most online library information is book or journal titles (although increasingly entire journal and periodical articles are available online) which can be withdrawn from the library shelves. Usually you have to be a student or staff member to access material from university libraries, while public library material is generally available free of charge to everyone with a library card. Some universities will give library privileges to members of the public for a monthly or semester fee, most include these if you register for a continuing education course.

Libraries are especially useful because they are run by librarians. Librarians are trained specialists in information management. They have a thorough knowledge and understanding of how their collections are organized and are familiar with the quickest route to the information you need. Most significantly, an important part of their work is helping you find what you are looking for. So if you need help learning to search for information, your first stop in a library should be the closest librarian.

Libraries, particularly university libraries, also offer short courses in search techniques. A student unfamiliar with how to look for information would find it is useful to take such a course early in the semester. This provides excellent resources for assignments and reinforces the search methods developed in this book.

LOCATING INFORMATION

While different libraries can use different software to organize their online catalogues, it is possible to provide general guidelines for information searches. Librarians will give you a brief overview on the characteristics of their system. In particular, spend a few minutes doing any search tutorials provide by the system.

Most library online catalogues have a **find menu** on their opening screen. This menu contains a list of fields such as **author, title, subject, numeric, keywords** or other entries. If you have the specific details of the material you are searching for, enter this information in the appropriate field. A list of search results, or **matches**, will appear. These can be refined by date, type of material or other criteria. You can also use a related records feature to produce material similar to the titles produced by your first search.

When quick searching by author, title, subject and numerics:

* Omit initial articles in titles (A, An, The, etc.).
* Enter words and numbers in exact order.
* Punctuation is optional, except for hyphens.

- Invert personal names, e.g., Cohen Leonard.
- Keep proper order for company names, e.g., Canadian National Railway.
- Spacing is important in numeric searches, e.g., BV 731 D1B96.

If you do not know exactly what you are looking for, begin by doing a **subject search** in the printed *Library of Congress Subject Catalogues* located in most libraries. Library subject-field searches are keyed to the terms of these catalogues. Once you have narrowed your search within the area you are looking for, then do a search from the subject field in the **find menu** of the online catalogue. If you cannot locate an approximate subject category, try your own keywords in the keyword field. **Keywords** describe as closely as possible what it is you are looking for. When you receive a search list, rapidly scan the titles, looking for the closest match to your topic.

Here are some useful hints for searching by **keywords**:

- Search any word(s) in any order.
- Search faster without articles and prepositions (a, an, the, and, of, etc.).
- Use Boolean operators AND, OR, NOT to refine a search (see below).
- Again, librarians are often helpful in suggesting the right key-word, especially when you're stumped.

BOOLEAN OPERATORS

To make your search more specific, use **Boolean operators** between words in a keyword search. Most search tools use these operators and others to help you refine your searches.

They are used by library catalogues and the Internet search tools discussed in the next chapter. Always used in upper case, the most common operators are:

AND   Use this operator to retrieve items in which both key words are present in the material you are looking for, e.g., cats AND dogs.

OR   Use this operator to retrieve items in which at least one of the key words is present in the material you are looking for, e.g., jazz OR blues.

NOT   Use this operator to specify that the word immediately following **NOT** must be excluded from the material you are looking for, e. g., (sun AND moon) NOT nasa. This example will exclude all items from the American Space Agency containing the words *sun* and *moon*.

OTHER RESOURCES

If you need the most recent information in a certain subject area, go to the appropriate **periodical** or **journal database** to begin your search. Journals are much more likely to be current than books, given the time it takes to write and publish a book.

Another important source of research information are **CD-ROMs**. Increasingly, libraries have a wealth of information in this format. The advantage of these resources is that the best also have multimedia features such as images, sounds and video. These sources have opening screens to speed access to the information they contain.

 The major advantage of university and public library searches is that the material you locate is highly reliable and comes from sources screened by expert librarians who attest to its authenticity. The disadvantage is no matter how extensive the library's holdings, much more information is available on the Internet.

Reading exercise #8

Start timer now.

The Mystery of the Extinction of the Dinosaurs

Trying to understand why the dinosaurs became extinct has become one of the great geological detective stories. Some recent findings from the small Mexican village of Chicxulub have given scientists new hope that the answer may soon be known.

The story starts a little over 15 years ago in the town of Gubbio, Italy, where geologist Walter Alvarez was collecting sediment from a layer of rock which marked the boundary between the Cretaceous and Tertiary time periods. Geologists had long known that this boundary was important because it marked a period in the Earth's history, some 65 million years ago, when almost half of all known species suddenly disappeared, including the dinosaurs.

Walter brought some of his sample back to the United States and his father, Nobel prize-winning physicist Luis Alvarez, analyzed it for any unusual chemicals. To their surprise, the sample showed a high concentration of the element iridium, a substance rare on Earth but common in meteorites. To make sure there was nothing unusual about the Gubbio sample, they analyzed other Cretaceous and Tertiary boundary strata from around the world. They found extra iridium in these samples as well. Using the average thickness of the clay as a guide, they calculated a meteorite would require a diameter of about 10 kilometres (six miles) to produce this much iridium.

If a meteorite that size had hit Earth, the results could explain the extinction of dinosaurs. The dust thrown up in the air would have caused major climatic changes to which many animals could not rapidly adapt. A major problem with this theory, however, was that a 10-kilometre meteorite would leave a very large crater, between 150 and 200 kilometres (93-124 miles) in diameter. While Earth has many impact craters on the surface, few are even close to this size.

Because 65 million years had passed since the hypothetical impact, scientists decided to shift the search underground. A crater that old would almost certainly have been filled in. Just by chance, a Mexican oil company drilling off the coast of Yucatan discovered what appeared to be a crater about one kilometre (0.6 miles) under the surface near the village of Chicxulub. When core samples were analyzed, they showed the crater to be about 180 kilometres (112 miles) in diameter and 65 million years old. Was this the cause of the dinosaurs' extinction? The jury is still out, but evidence strongly suggests that the case of the disappearing dinosaurs may finally be solved.

Stop timer.

Calculate your reading rate according to the Chapter one formula. The word count for this selection is 413.

*Reading rate:*_____

Comprehension exercise #8
Answer the following questions either true (T), false (F), or not mentioned (N).

1. Dinosaurs became extinct at the end of the Tertiary time period. _____

2. Some scientists believe dinosaurs where wiped out by volcanic action. _____

3. Iridium is a rare chemical common to meteorites. _____

4. A Mexican oil company discovered a large underwater crater off the coast of Yucatan. _____

5. The mystery of the extinction of the dinosaurs may never be solved. _____

*Comprehension rate:*_____

Interested in learning more about the dinosaurs and the possible causes of their disappearance? With access to a library catalogue database, select at least three keywords and the appropriate operators to narrow your search. How many matches did you get?

CHAPTER NINE

Searching the Internet

The Internet is an extended network of information-laden computers, the kind maintained by universities, large companies and Internet service providers. All of these are interconnected through telephone lines and fiber optic cables. These computers can transmit information between themselves from 35 countries around the world – almost instantaneously. With the right hardware and software, your computer connects to a service provider and connects into this network.

In many respects this vast digital storehouse of information is all about questions. What to do with this huge amount of information? How to access it? How useful is it? In order to make any sense of it at all you have to learn how to use it properly. Fortunately – in the absence of helpful librarians to guide your Internet searches – there are many useful software programs called **servers** such as **Telnet, File Transfer Protocol (FTP), Gopher, World Wide Web (www), Usenet**. These servers are designed to connect you to the information you need. The server we are going to concentrate on is the increasingly popular World Wide Web.

Remember that the most likely matches will be found on the first page or two of your search results.

Both the advantage and disadvantage of the Internet is the enormous volume of information available. However, unlike the library information, material on the Internet is not necessarily reliable. Anyone can post information on the Net, and they do. Beware! Check your sources for credibility. Check out the credentials of the Web site and the credentials of the author of any material located in this way.

SEARCHING THE WORLD WIDE WEB (WWW)

The Web has about 20 percent of the information available on the Internet and that percentage is increasing every day. It is rapidly becoming the most favored server. The innovative and distinguishing feature of the Web is its use of **hypertext**. Each document on the Web is a hypertext document with special words (usually colored and underlined), buttons and pictures that connect or **link** to other pages within the same document or to other Web sites. A click on the link takes you directly to the indicated page. The concept of "surfing" came from the fact that hypertext makes it possible to jump from page to page, or Web site to Web site, without knowing specific Web site addresses.

SOFTWARE REQUIREMENTS

To connect to the Web requires software called a **client program** or **browser**. The most popular browsers at the moment are **Netscape Navigator** or **Microsoft Explorer**. Both are excellent and do more or less the same thing. Both can be used to access most of the other servers mentioned here. The browser is used to bring the information you need from the links or Web site addresses.

SEARCH ENGINE WEB SITES

To find something on the Web, you must first connect to an appropriate server. These sites contain two kinds of search tools called **catalogues** and **search engines**. Some can be accessed through the search feature of your service provider. If your service provider does not offer this access, you can travel directly to search engine if you know the Internet address. Some of the most popular search tools, and their Internet addresses, are listed in the following chart.

Name	Type	Address	Features
Alta Vista	Search Engine	www. altavista.com	Very big; indexes all words
Open Text	General Catalogue w/Search Engine	www.opentext.com	Indexes all words
Yahoo!	General Catalogue w/Search Engine	www.yahoo.com	Organized by humans; not by a computer "crawler"; good search capabilities
HotBot	General Catalogue w/Search Engine	www.hotbot.com	Big; fast; finds specific Web page code; good help section
Infoseek	General Catalogue w/Search Engine	www.infoseek.com	Fast; brief abstracts; searches news, FAQs, E-mail
Excite!	General Catalogue w/Search Engine	www.excite.com	performs conceptual searches – finds "same as" pages

The other search engines index only the title, summary and keywords of a Web site. If you are searching for information on "diamonds," for example, you will get matches when "diamonds" appears in the title, but not if it appears in the body of the text.

The most comprehensive search engines are **Open Text** and **Alta Vista**. They do not just index Web page titles and summaries like **Yahoo!** and **Excite**, they index every word in every page. This is much more powerful, but also leads to more useless matches. Choose your criteria carefully and use all the search features to narrow your search and reduce the number of matches. An effective way to reduce the number of matches is to customize your search by first going through the subject categories, usually located on the opening page of a catalogue or search engine, before inputting your keywords.

If you think of the Internet as a huge book, **Yahoo!** performs like the table of contents while **Open Text** is like the index. Although every good book should have both a table of contents and an index, the index is much more detailed and makes it possible to locate specific information much quicker than the table of contents.

Another fast way to determine if the material you have located is what you are looking for is to click on **Edit** of your browser, select **Find** and enter your keywords. This will tell you how many times your subject keywords appear in the document and should give you an indication of their relevance to your needs.

SEARCH OPERATORS

No matter which search tool you use, it is important to be as specific as possible in defining your search terms, otherwise you could end up with millions of irrelevant matches. As mentioned in the previous chapter, most search engines and catalogues use various kinds of tools known as operators to help you refine your searches. The most common are the basic Boolean operators AND, OR and NOT.

There are other operators, such as plus (+) and minus (-), parentheses, quotation marks, wildcard symbols and others specific to individual search tools.

 Always take a few minutes to check out the Help or Search Hints pages of search tools to familiarize yourself with their operators before beginning your search.

NEWSGROUPS

Newsgroups are bulletin boards where people of like minds discuss topics of mutual interest. They do this by using **E-mail**. Depending on the group, it may contain cutting-edge discussion on a particular subject. However, the newsgroup may transmit a great deal of irrelevant and incorrect information. Check the reliability of the newsgroups on a particular subject to find the ones that meet your needs.

What follows are essential tips to help you search smarter and faster on the Internet.

- **Be accurate:** Make sure you have spelled your search parameters correctly. Do not use plurals; omit articles in front of titles and keywords.

- **Be precise:** Always try to be as specific as possible with keyword searches.

- **Every tool has different rules:** Remember every search engine is different and has unique rules for constructing searches. Always read the Search or Help screens of catalogues or search engines. These screens offer essential information about default settings, such as whether search criteria are upper/lower case sensitive.

- **Learn to use Boolean logic** and other operators like quotation marks and brackets. (Review the section on these operators in the previous chapter.)

- **Don't panic:** If you are overwhelmed by the number of matches you get with a specific keyword search, try redefining your keyword search again.

- **Always save your most useful Web sites** for future reference and speed of return. Use **Bookmark** for **Netscape** or **Favorites** for **Explorer**.

- **Avoid heavy traffic periods:** Noon to 3 p.m. is the peak time period on the Internet. The best time for quick searching is first thing in the morning or in the evening.

Applying the relevant search tips listed above, do a Web search for additional information on how to do research on scientific subjects. Do the search with both a catalogue like Yahoo! and a comprehensive search engine like Alta Vista. Select as precise keywords as possible and use appropriate operators to help refine your search. Skim through the titles and brief summaries of the search results and download the most appropriate entries for your needs for reading offline. Good luck!

Reading exercise #9

Start timer now.

Adapted from *The Reading Solution*, by Paul Kropp

Reading does not take place in a vacuum. It occurs only when it has a purpose, when it is useful, when it brings joy – and when it is connected with power. No child learns to read so he can someday savor a Robertson Davies novel. He learns to read to understand and control the world around him.

Carl Braun of the University of Calgary summed it up nicely when he was president of the International Reading Association: "I believe we need to remind ourselves about the potential of literacy for real empowerment – and the obverse, the estrangement, embitterment and the vast human potential that is laid waste as a consequence of illiteracy."

The framers of democracy in France, England and the United States understood very well the connection between literacy and power. The goal of literacy for everyone stems from democracy's need for involved, knowledgeable and empowered citizens. No wonder the first act of despots is to seize the mechanisms of print and put limits on personal expression. Yet our society, though we call it free and democratic, is today subject to forces that undermine both literacy and the easy access to books that should be a hallmark of civilization. As we enter the 21st century, I sometimes fear that reading – the goal of universal literacy – is in real danger unless all of us rally to defend it.

For the past 500 years, up until at least the 1960s, the progress of civilization has been accompanied by increasing levels of literacy. In most of Western Europe, for example, reading skills expanded from the clergy and aristocracy in the 16th century to include perhaps half the working class in the 18th century, to near-universal literacy (defined as the ability to sign one's name) by the end of the 19th century.

Unfortunately, the historical progress of literacy has been stalled in Canada and the United States since the 1960s. While basic decoding skills are stronger than ever and we now have a larger potential pool of readers, the actual percentage of adults reading is static or in decline. Serious literature and poetry are increasingly unread or connected more to academia than ordinary life. Even the newspaper, that emblem of revolutionary democracy for 200 years, is facing declining readership with its greatest losses among the young.

Some of the decline in adult reading can be explained by our shrinking leisure time and the competition of films, videos and television for the hours that remain. But I fear a more insidious cause – the entrenching of our current power structure and the despair of many who feel that nothing can be done to change it.

Literacy has always been a means to acquire power for those who haven't yet achieved it – the emerging middle class in the 18th century, immigrant groups in the 19th century, a wide assortment of groups and individuals in our century. For this reason, universal literacy was seen as a danger to established elites. In the words of one English pamphleteer: "Of all the foolish inventions and new-fangled devices to ruin the country, that of teaching the poor to read is the worst." Reading, books and literacy managed to put many more hands on the levers of power – until recently.

While I am not about to suggest that there is an active conspiracy against reading and the empowerment of full literacy, certainly something has happened to stall the progress of literacy in our time. As parents, we want our children to grow up to be literate, active, committed adults – to live better, richer lives than ours. Not every economic and political force in Canada has similar goals.

In the century to come, I do not fear for literacy, which will certainly survive for the educated elite. My fear is that real literacy will be the preserve of only a few, while many others will lapse into a passivity that saps their economic and political strength. As parents, we can't allow this to happen. Reading – real literacy – should be a birthright for all our children.

Stop timer.

Calculate your reading rate according to the Chapter one formula. The word count for this selection is 682.
*Reading rate:*_____

Comprehension exercise # 9
Answer the following questions either true (T), false (F), or not mentioned (N).

1. Children read to understand and control the world. _____

2. The original framers of democracy understood the relationship between literacy and power. _____

3. Newspaper readership is on the rise. _____

4. More books are being published than ever before. _____

5. The author believes there will be more book readers in the 21st century. _____

*Comprehension rate:*_____

Congratulations on completing this book and the practice exercises! If you have been recording the results of the exercises in the Appendix B – progress table, you should have noticed a steady increase in your reading speed and comprehension as you progressed through the book. If you consistently apply these new skills to everything you read from now on, not only will your reading speed increase even more, but you will also increase your reading pleasure throughout the rest of your life.

Twelve essential speed-reading tips

Maintain a positive attitude

Concentrate

Avoid distractions

Push yourself

Set goals

Always use a pacer

Practice

Always read with a purpose

Preview

Vary reading speed

Visualize, don't vocalize

Don't regress

APPENDIX A

Answers to comprehension exercises

Exercise	Answers				
1	1. T	2. F	3. T	4. F	5. N
2	1. F	2. N	3. T	4. T	5. T
3	1. F	2. T	3. N	4. F	5. T
4	1. T	2. T	3. F	4. N	5. F
5	1. F	2. T	3. T	4. F	5. N
6	1. T	2. N	3. T	4. F	5. T
7	1. F	2. N	3. T	4. T	5. F
8	1. F	2. N	3. T	4. T	5. F
9	1. T	2. T	3. F	4. N	5. F

APPENDIX B

Progress table

Reading exercises	Time in seconds	Words per minute (wpm)	Comprehension
#1	_____	_____	_____
#2	_____	_____	_____
#3	_____	_____	_____
#4	_____	_____	_____
#5	_____	_____	_____
#6	_____	_____	_____
#7	_____	_____	_____
#8	_____	_____	_____
#9	_____	_____	_____

BIBLIOGRAPHY

Speed Reading, by Tony Buzan, Penguin, 1991.

Improving Reading Comprehension and Speed, Skimming and Scanning, Reading for Pleasure, by Marcia J. Coman and Kathy L. Heavers, NTC/Contemporary Publishing, 1998.

Remember Everything You Read, by Stanley D. Frank, Times Books, 1990.

Finding It on the Internet, by Paul Gilster, John Wiley & Sons, 1996.

Web Search Strategies, by Bryan Pfaffenberger, MIS Press, 1996.

Speed Reading Made Easy: 6 Steps to Reading Excellence, by Arlyne F. Rial, Doubleday, 1985.

Speed Reading, by Robert L. Zorn, Harper Perennial, 1991.

Credits

First Nations of Canada. Indian and Northern Affairs, 1997 – Reproduced with the permission of Public Works and Government Services Canada, 1998.

Killer Whales. Dolphin Action and Protection Group, Fish Hoek, RSA.

"The Discovery of Champagne" and "The Invention of the Potato Chip" from *How Did They Do That?* by Caroline Sutton, 1984. Reproduced with permission the Williams Morrow & Company, Inc. 1998.

Halloween. Reproduced with the permission of Jerry Wilson.

The Hubble Space Telescope. Reproduced with the permission of the National Space Science Data Center, NASA.

The Mystery of the Extinction of the Dinosaurs from "Newton's Apple Teacher's Guide." Reproduced with permission of Twin Cities Public Television.

Adapted from *The Reading Solution* by Paul Kropp. Reproduced with the permission of the author.

NOTES & UPDATES

NOTES & UPDATES